Striking Steelhead

22 Years of Data & Lessons Learned
on the Clearwater
Back Trolling Lures from a Drift Boat

W0006954

MW01061959

by Dan Magers

Frank Amato
Publications
Portland

Dedication

*F*or the men and women who have volunteered their time and money to advocacy groups in Idaho and to the professional fishery managers—who have worked tirelessly to restore anadromous fish runs—devastated by the construction of eight dams between the Pacific Ocean and their natal streams 500 miles away in Idaho.

*F*or my favorite fishing buddy of the past 40 years, my wife Pamela... *Nobody* got more excited about a day on the river or line being peeled off a reel by a jumping steelhead than Pam.

All inquiries should be addressed to:
Frank Amato Publications, Inc.
P.O. Box 82112 • Portland, Oregon 97282
www.amatobooks.com • (503) 653-8108

All photos by Dan Magers unless otherwise noted
Title page by Mike McElhatton (www.digitalartsphotography.com)
Cover and book design by Tony Amato

SB ISBN-13: 978-1-57188-488-6   SB UPC: 0-81127-00333-4
HB ISBN-13: 978-1-57188-499-2   HB UPC: 0-81127-00345-7

Printed in China

1 3 5 7 9 10 8 6 4 2

Table of Contents

Foreword 6

Chapter 1   Background 8

Chapter 2   Steelhead Run A's & B's 11

Chapter 3   The Clearwater B-Run: Wild, Natural & Hatchery 18

Chapter 4   Clearwater Fish Factories: Wild, Natural & Hatchery .. 24

Chapter 5   Clearwater B-Run Timing 30

Chapter 6   Water Temperature is Almost Everything 37

Chapter 7   Hydraulics (where they live) 50

Chapter 8   Flow 62

Chapter 9   Methods and "The Method" 68

Chapter 10   The Lures, the Best Colors 71

Chapter 11   Time of Day 78

Chapter 12   Fishing Pressure, Weather Factors, Light 83

(I'm not superstitious, there's just no chapter 13 in this book)

Chapter 14   Drift Map 90

Chapter 15   Upper River Favorite Drifts 93

Chapter 16   Lower River Favorite Drifts 100

Chapter 17   Plan 105

Chapter 18   A Perfect Steelhead World: Top 60 Days 106

Chapter 19   Our Technique & Some Rambling Opinions 110

Chapter 20   Funny, Amazing and Just Plain Stupid 118

Chapter 21   The Six Best and The Ugly 122

A Steelhead's Top 22 Favorite Tricks 128
Friends and Relatives Who Fished With Me 129
Acknowledgements 130
Dan's Fish Log© Comments 131

Slimerocket launch.

Foreword

I have fished steelhead for 30 years and kept detailed records of the middle 18 years on Idaho's Clearwater River. I prefer big, aggressive, acrobatic steelhead the fall months provide on the Clearwater ("Slimerockets"). I pulled on the oars in my drift boat a few million times in my 22 years of Clearwater time, fully documenting 18 of those 22 years. I filled out a daily log sheet every evening when we returned from the river, logging the variables and fish we hooked.

My daughter Ginger filled over 18,000 cells with information while putting my records into a data base. Then she began the real job of teaching me how to use it. This effort resulted in being able to tabulate and sort the data I accumulated in 1,883 hours of driftboat time (avg. 2.5 anglers) while hooking 1,162 steelhead on Idaho's Clearwater River from 1988-2005.

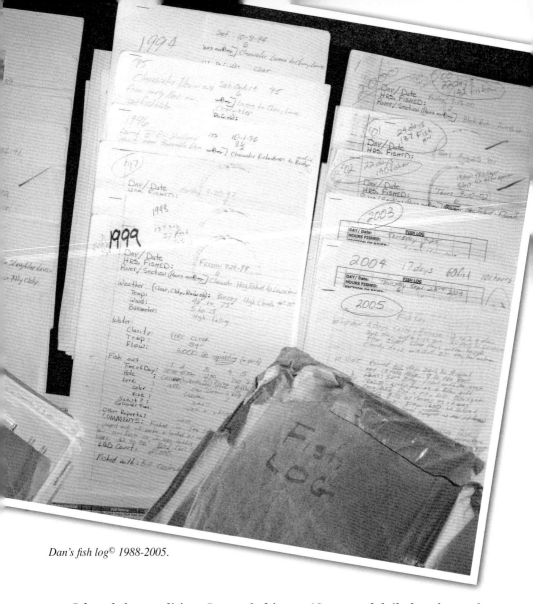

Dan's fish log© 1988-2005.

I found the conditions I recorded in my 18 years of daily log sheets that produced successful steelhead fishing on the Clearwater were also helpful understanding where fish might be on other rivers I fished in Oregon, Washington, and Alaska regardless of my method of fishing. I, like most other working people, had limited time to spend on the river and was looking to eliminate a lot of guess work. Did I succeed? You decide.

The presentation and my analysis of the data are here. This book was an afterthought suggested by a couple of my fishing friends. My guess (and hope) is that you will find something in this data that will save you a lot of time, increase probability and improve your catch rate—regardless of how you prefer to fish steelhead or what river you are addicted to anywhere.

Chapter 1

Background

*T*he sea-run rainbow trout or steelhead is the finest sport fish that swims in fresh water. Successful fishing for steelhead is also one of the most perplexing concepts to grasp for fishermen that have pursued other species of fish that are feeding. The learning curve on these incredible fish is steep, expensive and time-consuming. Prolonged exposure to every kind of imaginable weather and cold rocky rivers can be dangerous, as well. After a couple of trips to the wrong place at the wrong time, it became very apparent to me that 10% of the steelheaders catch 90% of the steelhead. It is the truth regardless of how they fish. What did they know that I did not know? I was determined to find out. I have always been lucky and this endeavor was no different.

I met Mitch Sanchotena, the steelhead guide at Mackay Bar on Idaho's Salmon River. Mitch was always gracious in sharing his knowledge about steelhead habits if someone cared enough to ask and was smart enough to listen to the answers.

My association with Idaho Steelhead & Salmon Unlimited had me rubbing elbows with some of the best steelhead fishermen in the U.S. and biologists from the Idaho Department of Fish & Game and the Columbia Intertribal Fish Commission. What an education.

I began fishing the Clearwater River in 1988 when I met one of ISSU's directors, John Kelly, who lived and guided on the Clearwater. This too was quite an education.

Mitch Sanchotena (right) tags a wild steelhead.

The Clearwater B-run steelhead are larger but have the same characteristics and habits of steelhead in other rivers. The rivers are as different as night and day.

Like most steelheaders, I tried just about every technique. Eventually, I found back-trolling lures from a drift boat to be the most exciting for me. So the data in this book is based on that technique. No debate here whether other methods may be as good or better or more fun. Other methods are better in certain water conditions. It is a matter of personal preference.

Most importantly, I learned the successful

Mike Smith, Me, John Kelly – a long time ago!

10% of the steelheaders check river flows and temperatures, know steelhead migration habits, have a working knowledge of hydraulics and fish accordingly. They changed the type of water they fish and tactics to fit the conditions regardless of their preferred method.

The information presented in this book is mostly quantifiable. Some of the information had to be subjective or my boat would have looked like a floating weather station. I set out to log conditions that would eliminate guess work and make more efficient use of the time I had to fish. What I ended up with is an enormous amount of data and a set of parameters that greatly increases probability under varying conditions.

The next four years 2006-2009, I only recorded hours and fish hooked which averaged 1 hour and 29 minutes per hook-up, including float time between spots. If the last four years of hours and hook-up information were to be included in the 18 years of full data, it would total: 22 years, 2,033 hours, 1,261 steelhead, 1.61 hours per fish or 4.34 fish per 7-hour day.

I am no expert. There are a handful of professionals on the Clearwater that spend many days from September through March fishing the variety of ways necessary due to changing water conditions and client requests that are most successful. When the conditions were tolerable for our preferred method of fishing steelhead, on average we did as well or better than anyone. Those conditions are documented in this book.

I believe this information is sorted meaningfully and will be quite useful on any river even though it was collected on Idaho's Clearwater. It certainly made us much more efficient. Steelhead fishing is not a science and nothing in here changes that. It is and always will be—fishing. However, this data proved to me that a person can increase the probability of hooking steelhead if they pay attention. Fishing the right hydraulics at tolerable flows and acceptable temperatures, in a likely stretch of river, dramatically improves hook-up rates. If someone had handed me this information 30 years ago, I would have saved months of time, lots of money and I would have hooked hundreds more steelhead.

Slimerockets "Data Collection Vessel".

Chapter 2

Steelhead Run A's & B's

Idaho is home to some of the most beautiful rivers in America, all flowing snowmelt from the western slope of the northern Rockies eventually to the Columbia River and on to the Pacific Ocean. Three of these rivers host steelhead runs. The Snake, the Salmon and the Clearwater all originate in designated wilderness or "roadless" areas and at some point along their path are designated "Wild and Scenic" by the U.S. Government. Their waters are pristine at their origin and to varying degrees less so as they wind their way through civilization. The Clearwater is the result of the confluence of the Selway, Lochsa, South Fork and North Fork Clearwater rivers. There is little development at their origins. At normal flow a person can stand up in the drift boat and look down into eight feet of water and see the bottom of the river. The Clearwater is appropriately named.

These three main river systems all had native, genetically distinct steelhead runs with different run timing prior to dam construction on the main stem Columbia and Snake rivers. Neither the Salmon nor main stem Clearwater are dammed.

The North Fork Clearwater is dammed at Ahsahka. This put hundreds of miles of upstream wild spawning and rearing habitat out of reach to fish. Dworshak National Fish Hatchery was built to mitigate the lost production of the submerged North Fork Clearwater River—now called Dworshak Reservoir.

Dworshak Dam supplies a regulated, varying flow of 50 (+/-)-degree water to a short stretch of what's left of the North Fork and on into the main-stem Clearwater River.

An Idaho Steelhead's Life Story

Idaho's summer-run steelhead migrate 400 to 500 miles from the Pacific Ocean into Idaho rivers. They enter the lower Columbia basin drainages in the late summer and fall (July-October) migrate to Idaho and winter over to spawn in streams from mid-April to late June. The female uses the gravel and cobble in a stream bed below a pool to dig a redd (nest). She displaces the gravel with her body and tail, and the male fertilizes the eggs as they are deposited. The

Dworshak Dam and the North Fork Clearwater.

female covers the eggs by moving upstream of the redd, using her tail and body again to displace gravel which is carried downstream and covers the eggs.

The eggs hatch in the summer and the young fish are on their own to grow in the stream. Most juvenile steelhead will spend two years in this stream environment before a biological change triggers their migration

Mark Smiley with an "A" run steelhead.

to the ocean. These out-migrating fish are called "smolt". A few will hang around another year and a few will "residualize" and not out-migrate at all. The juvenile fish that survive to the ocean will grow rapidly due to the abundant food supply.

When they mature and are ready to spawn the steelhead migrate back to the place they were born. This cycle takes three to five years to complete.

A-run steelhead spend a year in the ocean (one salt). B-run steelhead spend two, and some of them three, years in the ocean (two and three salt). The Snake River was the migration route of A-run steelhead to its tributaries and the Salmon and Clearwater river drainages produced primarily B-run steelhead.

A-run steelhead primarily spend one year in the Pacific and return 23-26 inches long and weighing approximately four to six pounds. These one-salt steelhead are about six percent of the returnees to the Clearwater.

B-run steelhead primarily spend two years at sea and return 31-34 inches long weighing approximately 10-14 pounds.

Bill Eggleston with a "B" run steelhead.

Mickey Turnbow with 37" & 43" "B's".

These two-salt steelhead represent approximately 91% of the fish returning to the Clearwater.

There are a few three-salt fish which are 37 inches plus in length, and account for the rare 20-pounder your friends catch. These three-salt steelhead represent approximately 3% of the fish returning to the Clearwater.

When more dams were constructed on the Snake River upstream from Lewiston, Idaho and fish-passage mitigation efforts failed, the decision was made to transplant the A-run Snake River steelhead into the Salmon River drainage through a series of out plants and hatcheries. As a result, today the Salmon River has mostly "A" and some "B" steelhead. This was not done in the Clearwater. Therefore, approximately 90% of the steelhead in the Clearwater are larger B-run (two- or three-salt fish).

The table below shows how the make-up of the run has changed a bit over the years. The first column is a 27-year average of the "age" of steelhead returning to the Dworshak National Fish Hatchery on the Clearwater River. The second column is the last 10-year average of the same data.

Age of Returns	27 Yr. Avg.	Last 10 Yr Avg.
One Salt (called "A"s)	10%	06%
Two Salt (Called "B's)	83%	91%
Three Salt (also called "B's)	07%	03%

Definitions: An "A" steelhead has historically been, and still is according to the Fish Passage Center (FPC), a fish passing Bonneville Dam prior to August 25th. Every fish passing Bonneville dam after August 25th is counted as a "B" steelhead.

The Idaho Department of Fish and Game (IDFG) has historical data that draws the biological line of "A" & "B" demarcation at a "78 centimeter fork length". Converting metric to imperial measurement and bio-speak to English, this means any steelhead with a length less than 30.71" from nose to the fork in the tail is an "A". Any steelhead greater than 30.71" from nose to the fork in the tail is a "B".

Not only are the agencies' definitions of a "B" steelhead different, they count them at different dams. FPC uses counts at Bonneville Dam before fish enter the Columbia River commercial fishery. IDFG uses counts at Lower Granite Dam, counting the fish left after crossing eight dams and the commercial fishery.

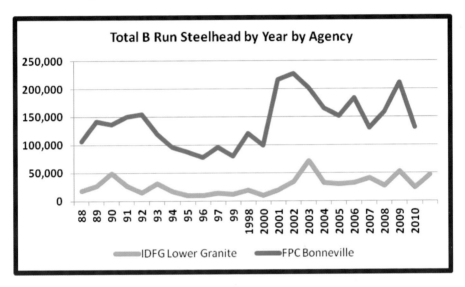

Uh, do you smell a potential management conflict here? I promised myself that I would not get into fish politics and I won't (except this once). But here is a table and chart (above) showing the differences in data that management agencies use to make decisions. The fish counts you see in the public media are virtually useless to predict fishing success on a day-to-day basis as are the records I kept of them. This is why they are not used in this book to sort data. Our 18-year trend shows gradual improvements in fish hooked even though the number of fish available to catch were the same or less. We hooked more fish in poor-run years in good conditions than vice versa.

So as my friend Gary Bush used to ask, "Why are half of our B's missing?" Since the overwhelming majority of the B's are headed to Idaho rivers, how could this be?

The discrepancy could be in the definition. If for instance half the B's are really A's that come over Bonneville after August 25 and the commercial fishery gets their 50%, then Idaho averages getting half of the half or 25% of the Bonneville count. Simple, eh? Not so fast.

| YEAR | Total Annual B Run Steelhead Counts by Management Agency Definition | | Bonneville to Lower Granite % |
	FPC "after 8-25" at Bonneville Dam	IDFG "78cm Fork Length" at Lower Granite Dam	
1987-88	78,180	18,323	23%
1988-89	88,488	26,595	30%
1989-90	115,579	49,100	42%
1990-91	87,368	26,814	31%
1991-92	123,292	15,554	13%
1992-93	139,300	31,351	23%
1993-94	88,058	17,685	20%
1994-95	78,367	9,409	12%
1995-96	78,192	9,688	12%
1996-97	68,220	13,856	20%
1997-98	82,020	12,126	15%
1998-99	67,838	19,760	29%
1999-00	100,576	9,643	10%
2000-01	89,915	19,959	22%
2001-02	196,171	33,851	17%
2002-03	193,678	71,599	37%
2003-04	130,176	32,572	25%
2004-05	132,986	29,958	23%
2005-06	121,505	31,961	26%
2006-07	151,738	40,847	27%
2007-08	89,311	26,611	30%
2008-09	132,185	52,641	40%
2009-10	158,199	23,338	15%
2010-11	108,014	45,666	42%
		Average	**24%**

Why don't we count them the same way at Bonneville that we do at Lower Granite? Certainly somebody in Portland, Oregon has a 78 cm tape measure. Methinks it may have something to do with the commercial-fishery harvest allocation.

The majority of the fall chinook salmon migrate up into the Columbia River system at the same time the B's migrate. Salmon sell for more money per pound than steelhead, so a concentrated effort is made by the commercial fishery to target salmon. Therefore the steelhead harvested are considered "incidental". The courts have mandated a 50%-50% split of the harvestable surplus steelhead between downstream commercial and upstream users. Once that 50% is reached in the commercial fishery, the nets come out of the water—meaning no salmon either. So the more B's that are counted, the longer the commercial salmon fishery.

So you, the agencies, the commissions, the states, the tribes, the U.S. government, the politicians and the courts can figure out if anyone has a vested interest in "over-counting" B's at Bonneville Dam. (No more fish politics).

Chapter 3

The Clearwater B-Run: Wild, Natural & Hatchery

There are three components (or origins) of the present-day Clearwater B steelhead run—wild, natural and hatchery. Idaho law requires the immediate release of all steelhead with an adipose fin, i.e. wild and/or natural steelhead.

Most hatchery fish have their adipose fins clipped prior to release for quick and easy identification upon their return as adults. (That's right, millions of smolt, hand clipped, one at a time, every year, prior to release.)

Un-Clipped Adipose Fin   **Clipped Adipose Fin**

MUST BE RELEASED

The biological definitions in Idaho are:

Wild steelhead are, "native fish, which have no history of reproductive introgression with hatchery or non-native fish or a limited amount unlikely to have had genetic effect. These fish are naturally produced without artificial intervention".*

Natural steelhead spawn, develop and return to remote upper tributaries of the drainage "but their parentage may include hatchery fish of native or non-native origin".*

Hatchery fish are hatchery produced. Again, most hatchery fish have their adipose fins clipped prior to release for quick and easy identification by fishermen who catch them upon their return.

*From 2006-2012 Idaho Department of Fish & Game Fish Management Plan

The way steel-head harvest is managed in the Columbia Basin (the Clearwater River being part of that system) is complex and conflicting. The runs over Bonneville Dam are "allocated" per previous court decisions to: 1. Ensure escapement of wild and natural fish into natural spawning habitat and to 2. Ensure escapement of hatchery fish to the menagerie of upstream hatcheries for production purposes to perpetuate the runs and 3. To allocate the remaining hatchery "harvestable surplus", half to Columbia Basin Tribes for subsistence

and commercial purposes and half to upstream users. Believe it or not, if hatchery returns exceed what is needed at the hatcheries, these fish are considered "wasted" by commercial interests and requests are made to increase commercial harvest.

Point being that releasing a hatchery steelhead in Idaho during an open season is not an act of conservation to protect future runs. If IDFG wants to plant some hatchery fish in an area to return and spawn naturally, they simply don't clip their adipose fins and, by law, they must be released. There are a lot of pictures in this book of hatchery steelhead that we kept if someone wanted to take fish home. We also released a lot of hatchery fish and I don't think I kept a fish the last five

Four hatchery Clearwater "B's".

Any steelhead with an adipose fin must be released.

years. This had nothing to do with protecting the resource, I just didn't want to deal with them.

All wild fish were released (by law) usually without even removing them from the water. A few were lifted out of the water for photographs then released—unharmed (like the cover fish). It's hard to photograph a lot of releases if you are the boat handler, photographer AND the fish releaser.

Calculated "harvestable surplus" estimates are conservative. Sport-harvest limits can be changed as the season progresses and more information is known. Allocation of this surplus between sport and downstream commercial interests is the source of a lot of bureaucratic and legal wrangling and even weekly meetings during the season.

Again, if harvest of hatchery fish is allowed, the only reason to release an adipose-clipped hatchery steelhead on the Clearwater is if you do not intend to use it. If hatchery returns look to be inadequate, regulations are changed to require the release of all steelhead—even of hatchery origin.

The fish going over the ladders at Bonneville Dam (BON) swim by a glass window where human beings actually sit and count each fish and record whether they are "wild" or "hatchery".

Page 21 shows the counts of B-run steelhead only—the past 25 years at Lower Granite Dam (LGR) by IDFG based on sampling.

LGR Dam B Steelhead counts adjusted by IDFG based on sampling
Hatchery origin includes fish with cliped and unclipped Adipose fin.
Run Year = July 1 to June 30   "B" fish = > 78 cm fork length

Run Year	Wild B's	% of total wild B's	Hatchery B's	Total B's
1986-87	5,477	14%	38,266	43,743
1987-88	5,240	40%	13,083	18,323
1988-89	4,587	21%	22,008	26,595
1989-90	8,110	20%	40,990	49,100
1990-91	4,483	20%	22,331	26,814
1991-92	3,198	26%	12,356	15,554
1992-93	5,778	23%	25,573	31,351
1993-94	1,790	11%	15,895	17,685
1994-95	2,231	31%	7,178	9,409
1995-96	1,338	16%	8,350	9,688
1996-97	1,645	13%	12,211	13,856
1997-98	1,324	12%	10,802	12,126
1998-99	2,302	13%	17,458	19,760
1999-00	885	10%	8,758	9,643
2000-01	2,885	17%	17,074	19,959
2001-02	3,174	10%	30,677	33,851
2002-03	13,623	23%	57,976	71,599
2003-04	7,261	29%	25,311	32,572
2004-05	4,774	19%	25,184	29,958
2005-06	3,480	12%	28,481	31,961
2006-07	1,633	4%	39,214	40,847
2007-08	2,916	12%	23,695	26,611
2008-09	5,661	12%	46,980	52,641
2009-10	4,396	23%	18,942	23,338
2010-11	10,456	30%	35,210	45,666
	108,647		604,003	712,650
	Avg. Wild	15%		

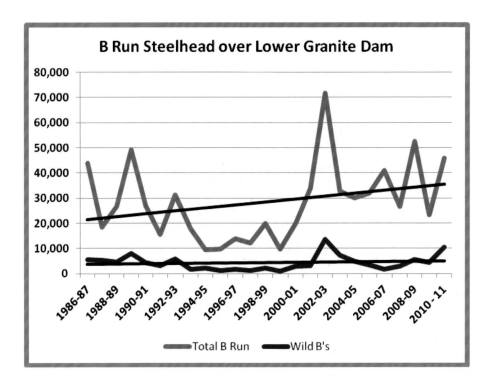

B Run Steelhead over Lower Granite Dam

Total B Run — Wild B's

The trend line (dark black line) of the total run is decidedly up the past quarter century due to big increases in 2003-2011. You will see below that during the time I kept the log (1988-2005), the trend line of the runs were flat. The 25-year trend line for the Wild B's is almost flat. So the increases from 2003-2011 are primarily hatchery production based. Over the past 25 years an average of 15% of the "B" steelhead entering the system were of wild or natural spawning origin. So why were 25%-40% of the steelhead we hooked and identified "wild"?

Two reasons...

• One is that we spent half of our time in the upper river where there would be a higher percentage "wild" population. The percentage of wild fish is higher since many hatchery fish have short stopped downriver returning to the hatchery.

• The second is that wild fish are more aggressive (they strike harder, fight harder, jump more and take longer to land too). Wild fish have to fend for themselves and survive in a wild environment. The natural selection process ensures only the strongest survive. Hatchery fish swim around in a protected environment waiting for the person in the gray shirt to throw them dinner and there's always enough to eat.

Question: Which hatchery steelhead make it back to the hatchery and are used for production of more steelhead?

Answer: The ones that didn't bite.

Fish are counted at the other seven dams upstream from Bonneville Dam as well. Typically, they are simply reported as "Steelhead" which includes both A's and B's. The information is available and why they are not separated in published reports is amazing to me. Generally, the trend of more fish over the last dam—Lower Granite—should equal a little better fishing. We found that using my log data to pick the most favorable conditions, and then fishing appropriately for those conditions, had a much more profound effect on B-run steelhead hook-up rates than how many total Steelhead (A's and B's) had passed Lower Granite Dam that year. Obviously, when conditions are right, more fish in the river will have a commensurate positive effect on hook-up rates.

The Perfect Steelhead

Once we evolved into catch-and-release-oriented, driftboat-based, fly-rod & reel, back-trolling snobs who didn't want to take fish home, we developed a definition for "The Perfect Steelhead". This is a 32+-inch wild steelhead that is in the air instantly upon hook-up, jumps three or more times, makes a couple reel-screaming runs across or up-river, comes un-hooked just as it gets to the boat and darts away.

"Many men go fishing all their lives
without knowing that it is not fish they are after."

—Henry David Thoreau

Chapter 4

Clearwater Fish Factories: Wild, Natural & Hatchery

Hatchery Steelhead

There are two major hatcheries on the Clearwater River. Located at the confluence of the main-stem Clearwater River and the North Fork of the Clearwater river, Dworshak National Fish Hatchery is considered one of the world's largest steelhead trout and spring chinook salmon-rearing facilities. The hatchery was built in 1969 to mitigate for the loss of the Clearwater River B-run steelhead trout as a result of the construction of Dworshak Dam. Additional construction was completed in 1982 under the Lower Snake River Compensation Program (LSRCP). The purpose of the hatchery is to mitigate for loss of summer steelhead and resident trout habitat after the construction of Dworshak Dam on the North Fork of the Clearwater River. Spring chinook production is to mitigate for dams constructed on the lower Snake River.

Dworshak National Fish Hatchery.

Photo Courtesy of Dworshak National Fish Hatchery

Clearwater Hatchery.

Clearwater Hatchery, along with its three satellite trapping and smolt acclimation stations, is the last of the Lower Snake River Compensation Plan facilities built by the U.S. Army Corps of Engineers in 1992. It is located on the north bank of the North Fork of the Clearwater River, 1.8 miles downstream from the Dworshak Dam. The hatchery raises spring chinook salmon and steelhead trout. The hatchery receives 3.5 million eyed steelhead eggs from Dworshak National Fish Hatchery for rearing. The three trapping and acclimation stations—Powell, Red River and Crooked River satellites—each over 120 miles upriver from the Clearwater Fish Hatchery, are required for the trapping and successful spawning of the returning adult salmon.

These hatcheries are necessary to provide the zillions of juveniles needed to ensure stock replenishment and sport fishing. There is an approximate 90% mortality rate of all Clearwater juveniles during outmigration through eight dams. When returning adult loss is added, about 2% make it back. Without hatchery operations, there would be nothing but a catch-and-release fishery for wild steelhead—if that. Contrary to popular opinion, there is mortality associated with catch-and-release fishing.

Pit tags are tiny electronic chips inserted into the fish that help biologists track movement. Some smolt are pit-tagged and released and some returning adult fish are taken from the ladders and tagged then tracked as they cross subsequent dams. Antennae affixed to vehicles drive the highways along the river and record the information. (This will provide an interesting piece of information later in the book.)

Common wisdom is that juveniles are released from the hatchery gate and return there. The Clearwater Hatchery doesn't even have a hatchery gate to release fish from nor for adults to return to. Eyed eggs are transferred in, grown and all moved out for release in other locations. As a result of this "common wisdom", most fishermen fish downriver—below the two hatcheries thinking that's the only stretch of river where they can catch a keeper. "Everything upriver is 'wild'."

Here is a list of juvenile hatchery fish, most with clipped adipose fins, (keep-able fish) that were planted in tributaries of the Clearwater River in 2006-2010. This program is ongoing.

Granted, there are more fish released directly from Dworshak National Fish Hatchery than these totals to follow but there are many hatchery fish in the upper river other than strays.

Clearwater River Drainage			Number
Location	Date	Species	Stocked
Clear Creek	4/20/2010	Steelhead	144,934
Crooked River	4/14/2010	Steelhead	86,743
	4/17/2009	Steelhead	73,287
	4/9/2008	Steelhead	72,112
	4/7/2008	Steelhead	144,557
	4/15/2007	Steelhead	83,811
	4/12/2007	Steelhead	151,296
	4/13/2006	Steelhead	148,652
	4/11/2006	Steelhead	76,604
Lolo Creek	4/28/2009	Steelhead	50,250
	4/21/2008	Steelhead	45,608
	4/19/2007	Steelhead	52,415
	4/26/2006	Steelhead	50,020
Meadow Creek	4/18/2008	Steelhead	31,429
	4/17/2007	Steelhead	28,050
	4/25/2006	Steelhead	24,954
Mill Creek	4/20/2009	Steelhead	25.354
	4/18/2008	Steelhead	31,429
	4/17/2007	Steelhead	28,338
	4/25/2006	Steelhead	24,954
Newsome Creek	4/15/2010	Steelhead	107,312
	4/20/2009	Steelhead	25,354
Red River	4/12/2010	Steelhead	153,644
	4/13/2009	Steelhead	131,803
	4/11/2008	Steelhead	82,930
	4/10/2008	Steelhead	163,580
	4/15/2007	Steelhead	251,646
	4/24/2006	Steelhead	47,029
	4/14/2006	Steelhead	192,125
S.F. Clearwater River	4/19/2010	Steelhead	362,327
	4/16/2009	Steelhead	263,999
	4/14/2009	Steelhead	265,589
	4/15/2008	Steelhead	247,619
	4/13/2007	Steelhead	272,819
	4/17/2006	Steelhead	289,508
		Total	4,206,752

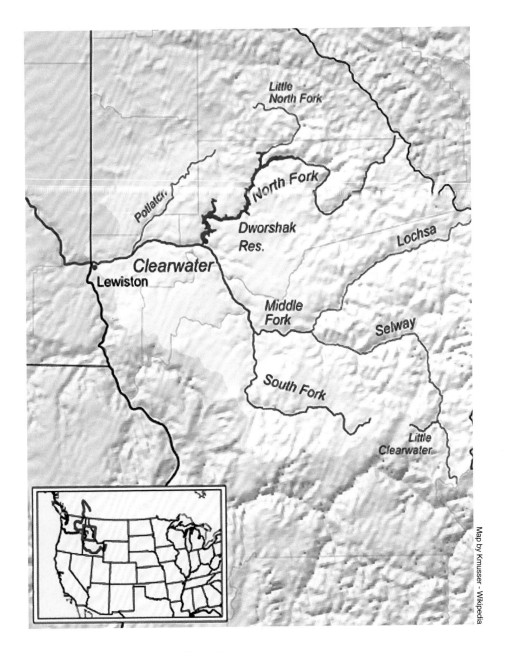

Map by Kmusser - Wikipedia

Wild & Natural Steelhead

Idaho manages the Selway and Lochsa rivers as wild steelhead rivers.

From the IDFG 2006-2012 Fisheries Management Plan:
"Geographic location of primary wild populations of salmon and steelhead in the Clearwater River: Lower Clearwater tributaries excluding Lolo Creek drainage, The Lochsa River Drainage and The Selway River Drainage."

The Selway

The Selway River is approximately 100 miles in length from the headwaters in the Selway-Bitterroot Wilderness to the confluence with the Lochsa near Lowell to form the Middle Fork Clearwater River.

The Lochsa

The Lochsa River is 70 miles long from its headwaters near Powell Ranger Station in the Bitterroots to Lowell, Idaho where the Lochsa joins the Selway River to form the Middle Fork Clearwater River.

Photo Courtesy of Kevin Colburn - www.americanwhitewater.com

The South Fork Clearwater

The South Fork Clearwater River flows 45 miles from its head waters near Red River Hot Springs to its confluence with the Middle Fork at Kooskia, Idaho. The South Fork is managed for "Natural" fish production. All of the out-plant locations in the previous table are in the South Fork or its tributaries, except Lolo Creek.

Considering Clearwater fish production and my previously stated bias toward wild fish, looking at the map on page 26, where on the map would I want to fish? If you chose the stretch from the mouth of the South Fork down to the North Fork at Ahsahka, you would be correct. There are three other reasons we spent as much time in the upper river as possible.

First, the Middle Fork Clearwater above the Orofino bridge is no-motors water during steelhead season. This spreads fishing pressure and reduces user conflicts. The upper river is pretty skinny anyway at lower flows, especially for power boating, so it's almost a natural dividing line.

Second, steelhead stray—a lot. Many years ago IDFG asked some professional guides to participate in a tagging study of fish they caught. Mitch Sanchotena agreed to do this at Mackay Bar on the Salmon River. He tagged and recorded locations where he caught some of these fish then returned them to the river. Some of the fish Mitch tagged were 35 miles above the hatchery they ended up going back to in the spring—which incidentally was the wrong hatchery. (Also of interest were a couple wild fish he caught more than once.)

Third, remember the "pit tag" reference? Some years ago when fishing the upper river we would see a small pick-up drive slowly up and down the highway that had what looked like a TV antennae mounted in the back. This apparatus was reading electronic information being emitted

Photo by Kevin M. Becker - www.flickr/kmboise

by the pit tags in some fish. We stopped one day when we saw the operator pulled over eating lunch. He also confirmed that hatchery fish will overshoot their target by miles if water conditions are favorable.

That worked for me. I will take the overshoots, out plants, no-motors water, higher concentrations of wild fish and reduced fishing pressure—above Orofino—provided the conditions were acceptable, which they only were about half the time.

Chapter 5

Clearwater B-Run Timing

*A*ll Clearwater steelhead must pass eight dams on the Columbia and Snake Rivers to reach Idaho's Clearwater River. This has slowed the run timing a bit - according to old timers—but makes sense. The first of those dams is Bonneville Dam on the Columbia.

Please notice two things on this graph. First, the noticeable spike up around August 10th and then back down bottoming around August 25th. This first wave of fish are primarily A's. Then the spike back up in the same line when a second wave of fish begin passing Bonneville around August 25th. These are primarily B's.

Second, there are a LOT more fish in the first wave than the second due primarily to higher A-run hatchery production and also a larger geographical area of A-run distribution in the basin for wild and natural spawning.

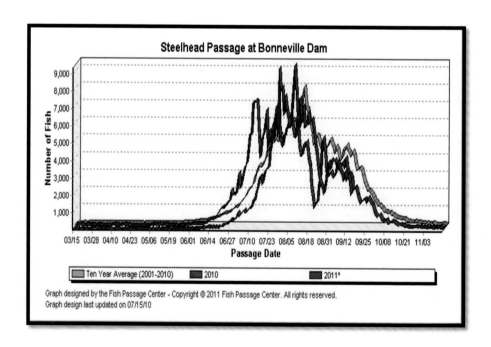

Graph designed by the Fish Passage Center - Copyright © 2011 Fish Passage Center. All rights reserved.
Graph design last updated on 07/15/10

This is not exact. Some two-salt steelhead cross Bonneville before August 25th and some one-salt steelhead cross after the 25th. This line is getting grayer. So how long does it take for the B's to get to the Clearwater? It all depends on water temperature and flow in the Columbia and Snake Rivers. A cool wet September will move fish upriver a lot faster than a hot dry

James Gross and Pamela Magers, not their better sides but you get the picture.

September. The last Dam is Lower Granite.

Looking at the 10-year average comparison of the two charts, from peak to peak it takes about 40 days for a steelhead to "convert" or to get from Bonneville Dam to Lower Granite Dam. But that's the 10-year average of hot, dry years and cool, wet years.

Of most interest, there is a new part of the FPC web site at http://www. fpc.org/ that has a link called "Travel Time". In summer 2011 we had record

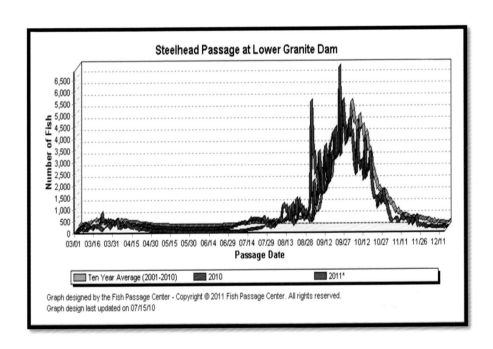

snow pack, record high river flow and cool, wet early summer weather. The Columbia River temperatures were in the 50's and early "Travel Times" for steelhead from Bonneville to Lower Granite was 21-28 days. I did not have this data when I was recording information. But the 10-year average dates you see in the graphs correspond almost exactly with our 10-year average dates when catch rates would get much better.

Over the years, October 6th was the mean date our catch rates started to improve dramatically. I look at these graphs and it is obvious why. The last four years, if it was an average flow year, I did not even get to the Clearwater until October 5th. If we had high cool flows, I was there in mid-late September. The FPC's Travel Time link is a real tool for timing an early season trip.

There is a lot of opinion as to whether October or November offers the best opportunities.

My 18 years of fishing data shows the following:
Since we generally fished more days in October than November, the only fair comparison is the average boat hours per fish. The average boat hours per fish were 1.90 in October and 2.22 in November.

In only four of 17 years was our November fishing better than in October—despite the fact there are more fish in the Clearwater in November. These averages though are skewed by three years of abnormal October flows. In glancing back at a couple of these slow Octobers, there were water

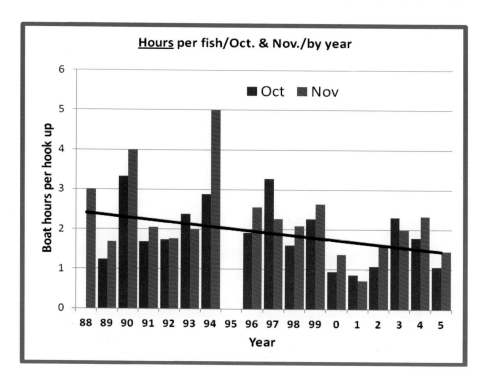

anomalies, either abnormally high or low flow that skewed October results down. If I throw those three years out, the October rate falls to 1.87 boat hours per fish and the November rate jumps to 2.38. There should be more fish in the river and there are usually more high-water flow issues in November. But if flow was too high, we simply didn't fish. As I think you will see, water temperature, harvest and flow are the reasons we did better in October.

I threw out some special situations data **in the above chart** for October and November. Situations like hole hopping (creaming the best spots we had found that year) putting the boat in and out of the best spots on a given day (a lot of work). This chart data is based on full-day floats.

There are also some special situations in August/September and in December discussed in the temperature chapter later where catch rates were quite high and lowered the overall average. I did however include these special situations in overall hook-up numbers and in boat hours/ per hook-up/per drift Chapters 12 & 14—which is why they are both lower. Right, wrong or subjective, that's how I sorted it.

In 1995, the B-run count was so low there was a question as to whether there would even be enough hatchery fish to make "escapement" in the hatchery. Therefore, the keep season was closed—catch and release only of all Clearwater steelhead—even hatchery fish. We fished 29 hours in seven days that year and hooked 27 steelhead. Few fish, fewer fishermen, great fishing—1.07 hours per fish.

In 2001, we fished 12 days before October 20th and hooked a fish every 1.54 boat hours—great fishing. Rain blew the river out and kept it that way until November 3rd. We fished a four-day period November 4-7 and in 28 hours of fishing hooked 39 steelhead— that's .72 boat hours per fish...one every 45 minutes. Be an opportunist.

Doug Hayes and Tom Myers.

Question: As the years passed and our hours per fish were falling, were we getting better or were there more fish?

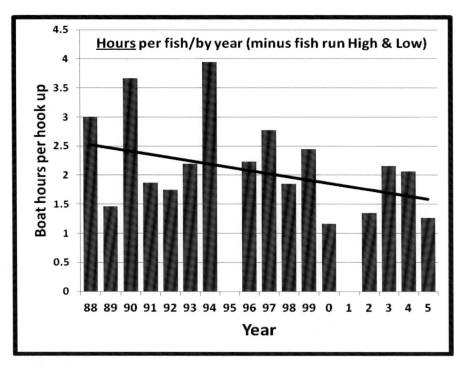

In looking for patterns or trends in the data, obviously our catch anomalies like 1995 and 2001 mask the real deal, as do total LGR Dam

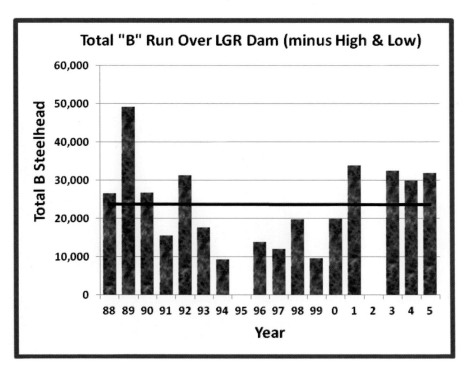

B-run steelhead count anomalies like 1995 and 2002. (I told you some of this was subjective). So I decided to throw out the two extremes in each to get a better picture.

You can see from the thick black trend lines (the computer drew the trend lines—not me) on the charts that our hook-up rate dropped from approximately 2.5 hours per fish down to 1.5 hours per fish during this 18-year period while the number of fish in the river stayed basically the same.

We had 27 El Skunko's total in the log. Sixteen were in the first four years, 12 in the last 13 years. There has been zero in the last four years (2006-2009) I fished catch-and-release only that are not in the log.

In addition, 34 of the "Best 60 Days" were in the last six years I kept records (2000-2005), meaning only 26 Best Days were in the first 12 years (1988-1999).

Using this information was paying off. We were hooking almost two fish more per seven-hour day when I ended the log book than when I started it.

Of course these charts beg the question why the runs are not increasing with all the money and effort being expended? The answer is they are . . . now. Look at the chart below at the increases in run size the past eight years and pay particular attention again to the thick black trend line. (Remember, I stopped recording data in 2005).

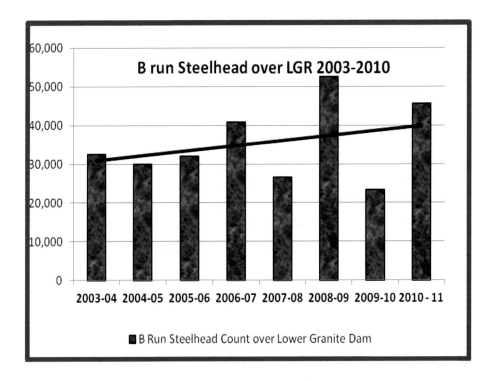

Perhaps flow regimes, collection and barging of smolt at Lower Granite Dam and other efforts are paying off. Big snow pack years don't hurt anything either.

A double, a rare event… and an even rarer picture of one.

Chapter 6

Water Temperature is Almost Everything

*T*here are two life-altering water temperature events in the world of steelhead. 70 degrees F. (21 C) is borderline lethal. As a result, steelhead do not feel very good when the water is in the mid-60's and seek out cooler water where they feel better. Below 40 degrees F. (5C) steelhead are all but dormant (yeah, some may bite and swim around the boat before they roll over but they're not Slimerockets). In the middle is 55° F. **Here is a graph** of October and November average water temperature on the upper river at Orofino from the USGS. (It's only published in degrees Celsius so a conversion chart is below it).

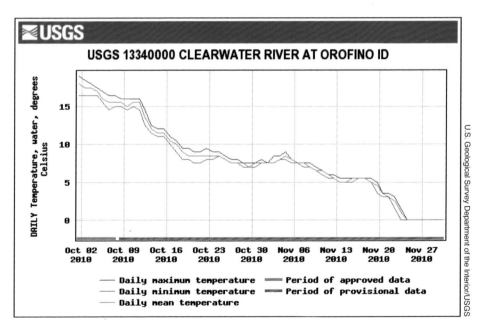

Degrees C	0°(C)	5°(C)	10°(C)	15°(C)	20°(C)	25°(C)
Degrees F	32°(F)	41°(F)	50°(F)	59°(F)	68°(F)	77°(F)

Sometime in the first week of October we get into the 50's. Sometime around mid November we fall below 40 and our back-trolling method of fishing is not near as effective.

I decided I needed to check my 18 years of recorded water temperature readings with the preceding **USDS graph above.**

Average Water Temp. F	U.S. Geological Survey	My Data Averages
October	**49.64**	**49.46**
November	**38.48**	**40.96**

I was pretty close in October because I fished the entire month. Why the discrepancy in November? I rarely fished when the water got below 40° F. so generally had few entries in the log the last week of November to pull my average down when water temperatures would fall off the cliff.

In the 22 years I kept catch-and-release records, we fished 91 days between October 1-14. Temperatures ranged from 42-58 degrees F. Both mean and average water temperature was 50° F. for this period. The bars show you that when the water temperature was between 42-58 degrees, we (2.5 anglers) averaged 3.9 fish per day. You will also notice how fast the catch rate fell off when water temperatures fell below this temperature band. Early October cold snaps causing a rapid fall in water temperature turned the fish off.

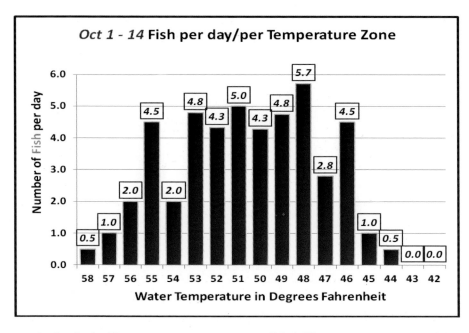

It also looks like my temperature gauge didn't like to say "54". So pull the 55 bar down a bit and 54 up a bit and you get the picture.

October 15th-31st

In 18 years of records for October 15-31, we fished 94 days. Water temperatures ranged from 40-53 degrees F. Average water temperature was 46.6° for this period. The bars show you that when the water temperature was between 40-53 degrees, we (2.5 anglers) averaged almost 3.5 fish a day hooked. The hookup rate went down with four changes in conditions:

Marshall Jacobs with an early October fish about to be released.

1. It was two weeks later.

2. More fish were entering the river every day.

3. The water was 3.4 degrees cooler.

4. Fishing pressure was much higher (because the season was open) and fish are being removed from the river (the hatchery fish that "bite").

With more fish in the river, does water temperature or fishing pressure cause the fall off in catch rates? You decide.

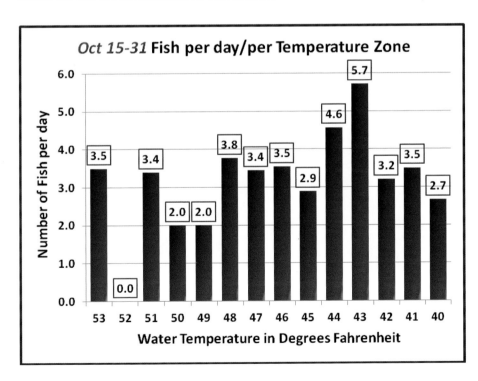

November

In 18 years of records for the entire month of November, we fished 100 days. Water temperatures ranged from 35-47 degrees F. Average water temperature was 42.1 degrees for this period. The bars show you that when the water temperature was between 35-47 degrees, we (2.5 anglers) averaged 3.0 fish a day hooked up. The hook-up rate went down again with four changes in conditions:

1. It was a month later.
2. The days get shorter.
3. More fish entering the river every day (until water drops below 40°).
4. The water was 4.5 degrees cooler.

Late October - Bill Eggleston.

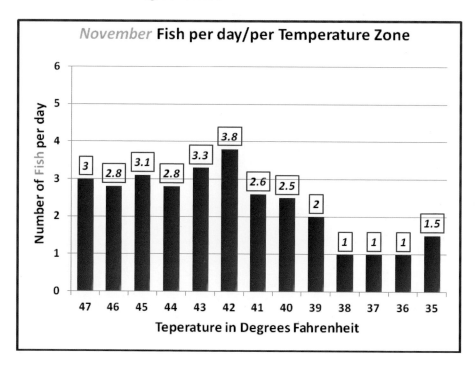

November fishing with George Whitaker (left) and Chris Oakes (right).

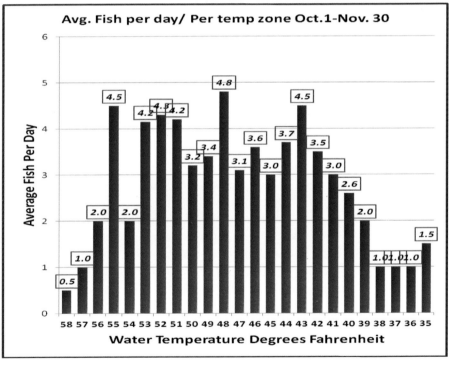

Putting them together for the entire period of October 1-November 30: Optimal = 42-55 degrees. Could it be any clearer? You can see why I didn't fish much in water below 40° F. What about the other days in August (yes, August) September and December?

Special Situations: August-September, December

These special situations significantly lowered the total boat hours per fish of the entire 18-year period.

August-September: 207 hours/157 hook-ups = 1.31 boat hours per fish.

August was a special-situation fishery for us. The last few days of August have afternoon air temperatures in the 90's. And as the charts have shown, the majority of the B's just started heading toward the Clearwater River a day or two before. Usually, the Corps in conjunction with the biological community will dump 5,000-10,000 CFS of 50-degree water from the bottom of Dworshak Dam to cool the water downstream and break the thermal blocks to fish passage. The A-run fish headed up the Snake River to the Salmon River really like this and would pull into the Clearwater and party in the lower stretches. The holes in the lower Clearwater (we fished from Upper Hog Island to Steelhead Park) would be full of nice fresh A-run and a few B-run steelhead. Problem with this was it is difficult to row a drift boat all day in 90-degree temperatures at 10,000 CFS.

September starts off in the August category and ends in the early October group. The upper river (above Orofino) natural flow is usually at its annual low and water temperatures at their annual high. After the late August, early September Dworshak dump to cool the rivers, 50-degree flows from Dworshak seemed to have been managed so that main-stem Clearwater flow was 2,900-3,000 CFS and water temperature averaged 52 degrees. Under these lower flow and slightly cooler water and air conditions we did well on the Peck-Lenore and Lenore-Cherry Lane drifts. The majority of fish we caught during this period were A's that partied too hard during the dump. Of course, if a cooler, wetter September happens, it just makes things better, faster and the fish get bigger faster too.

December: 69 hours/71 hook-ups = .91 boat hours per hook-up. December is REAL iffy. One December for whatever reason they were dumping Dworshak at about 12,000 CFS (remember 50+/- degree water). So we went into the upper river (34-degree water) and rowed down to the point where these two flows met. Fish won't leave 50-degree water to enter 34-degree water—even if that is where they are headed to spawn. We probably hooked 80 steelhead and landed 49 (I was only logging fish to the boat that year) in several trips there. Another year in December we had a warm wet-weather pattern that lasted for days, broke the ice off the upper river, raised flows and water temperatures into the 39-degree range. This big increase made the ole B's lying under the ice very happy even though it was still only 39. We rowed down to a tailout on the upper river, anchored, let the lures out and landed 5-6 fish every 4- to 5-hour trip. Regular fishing in sub-39-degree water in 30-degree air temperatures resulted in, maybe, one fish per day.

We have established 40-58 degrees as the broad water temperature range to hook steelhead, with 42-55 being optimal—The Zone. Where would a person find these conditions on the Clearwater? The answer is not nearly as simple as one would think. And on the Clearwater, water temperature is only about half weather dependent.

There are roughly two halves of the Clearwater River, upstream and downstream of Ahsahka, Idaho. These two sections are widely referred to as the "upper river" and "lower river". Technically, the main river upstream from Kooskia is the Middle Fork Clearwater River. Everything downstream from Kooskia where the South Fork Clearwater enters the Middle Fork Clearwater is the Clearwater River.

John Kelly.

This is important: The Clearwater River below Ahsahka (lower river) can be cooler or warmer than above Ahsahka (upper river) due to discharge from Dworshak Dam.

The picture on the right shows this in detail.
Dworshak Dam (way top left) discharges a constant but varying flow of 50-degree water into a small reach of what is left of the North Fork Clearwater (the left river). The North Fork then flows almost immediately into the main Clearwater River (the right river) creating a much larger Clearwater River (flowing out the bottom). Dworshak Hatchery is on the point where the two rivers and their different water temperatures come together. The Clearwater Hatchery is across the North Fork on the left.

The following three graphs show the past nine-year daily average water temperatures of the upper river (at Orofino) and the lower river (at Peck).

Steelhead are not prone to leaving cool water where they feel good to enter warmer water (unless the cool water is below 40°). So in a "normal" September, there will be more fish to exercise (catch and release) in the lower river (from Ahsahka downriver). Cool weather and rain can and often does change everything in September.

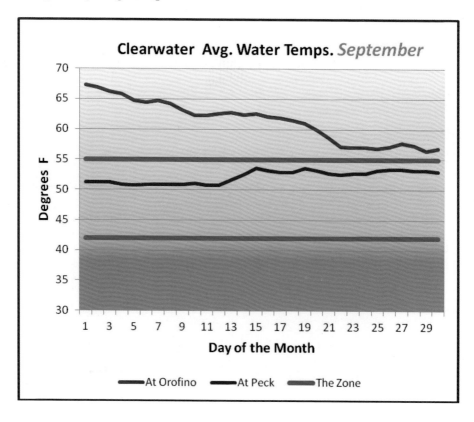

WATER TEMPERATURE IS ALMOST EVERYTHING

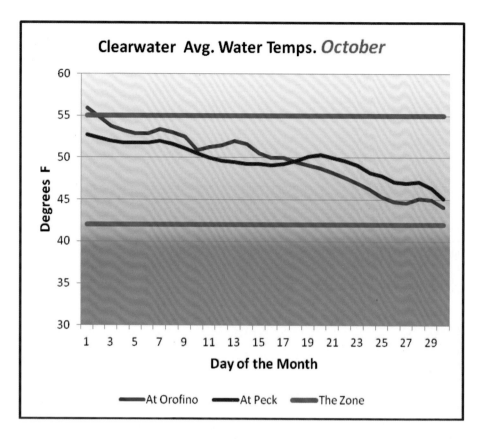

Clearwater Avg. Water Temps. *October*

October brings cooler water and a water temperature flip-flop about mid month. You could fish either stretch but there would still be more fish in the lower river. On average, about the 18th, the upper river (above Ahsahka) should turn on as water temperatures in the two sections reverse and fish enter the cooler water up river. This is why we loved October—lots of river to fish because water temperatures were in the optimal zone all month on both sections. Please remember these are nine-year averages and few years are average.

In November, the fishing should be really good in the upper river until water temperatures drop below 40° which historically has been about November 7-8. Then according to the graph, fish the lower river until about Thanksgiving, then go home and watch football. Steelhead lose Slimerocket status to me in water colder than 40°.

Remember, these graphs are averages of the last nine years. Unusual weather patterns can flip-flop these lines on the graph—and usually do. As you can see, Dworshak Dam flows act as a big heater or cooler to lower river temperatures depending on what nature is doing to the upper river.

You can save yourself some drives in the wrong direction and some walks down to the river with thermometer in hand by looking at the USGS Water

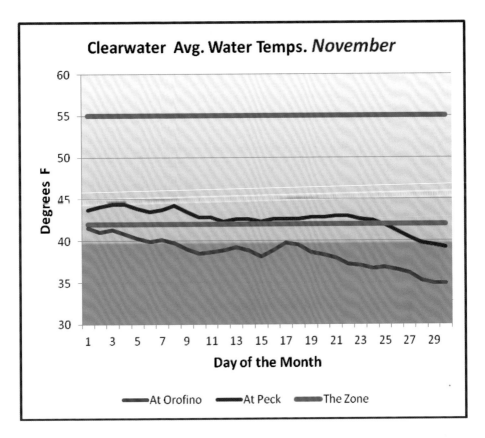

Clearwater Avg. Water Temps. *November*

Degrees F — *Day of the Month*

━━At Orofino ━━At Peck ━━The Zone

Data website and getting the Orofino and Peck temperatures (and flows) before picking your stretch of river (upper or lower). http://waterdata.usgs.gov/nwis

> You must be cognizant of water temperature—not just to pick the stretch of river that is most probable—but to tell you where in a hole a steelhead is most likely to be.

Partially Documented Opinion

There is little doubt in my mind that a steelhead is more aggressive in the upper ranges of the optimal temperature band meaning they will move further to strike a lure.

I was standing on the Salmon River at the mouth of a major tributary casting spoons in extremely clear 52-degree water. I hooked a fish which ran into the hole at the mouth of the tributary. I was standing on a rock about four feet above the water surface and could see the fish swimming around with the spoon in its mouth—and two others chasing it. When I pulled the fish in closer, the other two appeared to be trying to take the spoon from the hooked fish.

In another instance on the Clearwater, we hooked a fish in some fast 53-degree water at the very top of a hole. I was not far from calm water and moved the boat in there. My friend Mike Smith was reeling his lure in to get out of the way and as he was lifting the lure from the water a steelhead attacked and took Mike's lure with it. More than once in warm water I have had my fishermen remark that a fish had followed the lure in. This never happened in colder water.

The warmer the water, the faster the current we fished. I'm talking about starting to row in the bottom of a rapid as hard as possible so the lures were working as they dropped over the edge of the top of a hole. The two fishermen in front better have a tight grip as these are some of the most violent hits there are.

As the water cools a little, steelhead seem to back down a little in the hole or move over to the seams of the fast current. In 40-degree and less water they are in the slowest positive current in a hole and right along the edges of (but not often in) back eddys. We hooked a lot of steelhead in 40-42-degree water temperatures while anchored in slow current just fast enough so the lure would still dive and make the rod tip twitch.

I fished tailouts in all water temperatures, but even then, fish were in the slower portion up higher in the tailout in cold water and further down in the faster stuff in warm water. I'm sure you get the point . . . your probabilities rise if you do not waste time fishing frogwater hydraulics in 50-degree water temperatures or rapids in 40-degree water temperatures.

There is a reason for this. Steelhead don't eat once they enter fresh water. "Ah contraire," you say. "Why do you use shrimp tails and we catch them drifting eggs?" I think it is smell or a conditioned feeding response from their recent past. Or we just irritated them with something that happened to have bait on the hook that was bouncing along the bottom.

No question they bite baited hooks better than not, particularly in colder water. But I have cleaned more than my share of Idaho steelhead and never found anything in a stomach and, in fact, most of the stomachs just tapered down to a point. And I do not recall ever having to dig one of our single barbless hooks out of a steelhead's throat.

These are not coastal steelhead that can come in fresh from the salt with a full belly, spawn and go a few miles back. Idaho steelhead have one shot to spawn and they lay under the ice or in ice water all winter before continuing on to spawn in spring. Since they do not eat, they conserve energy when the water gets cold and do not chase lures like they do in warmer water. Thus, they find the slowest possible current, the hydraulics of tailouts and the bottom of the river to preserve energy in cold water. Yes, you can catch them in cold water—if you hit them right in the kisser with your offering. This is why our back-trolling method is inferior to deep bait-fishing in water below 40 degrees F.

Frog water on the Clearwater.

Steelhead are cold-blooded, meaning their internal body temperature changes as the surrounding temperature (water) changes. Any wonder why they are lethargic at 40 degrees and have a headache at 65 degrees?

When you think about it, The Zone temperatures should be no real surprise. The water temperature in the tributaries where steelhead spawn and rear in spring and summer is between 45-55 degrees F. The water coming from the bottom of Dworshak Dam and into both the Clearwater and Dworshak hatcheries is 50° F +/-. Pacific Ocean temperatures range from 49-55. Any wonder why steelhead are happy in 45-55-degree water?

Water temperature is almost everything.

Chapter 7

Hydraulics (where they live)

*Hydraulics: A branch of science concerned with the practical applications of flu-
ids and liquids in motion such as the flow of liquids in rivers, and channels . . .*

—Wikipedia

I am not a hydraulics engineer and most people reading this book are not either. Most hydraulics in a river that hold fish are invisible to fishermen. A
depth finder is imperative to see a lot of what we can't. **I decided to have diagrams drawn** of what types of hydraulics we found that held migrating fish in the
Clearwater River. I researched a lot of open-channel hydraulic flow information,
conglomerated it and then added our Clearwater experiences. The results are
diagrams from a fisherman's perspective with some good technical background.

In our context, "hydraulics" is a synonym for the steelheads' comfort zone,
i.e. holding water, water comfortable enough to cause a migrating fish to pause…
maybe stop and rest… comfortable enough to defend and become "biters". I believe steelhead move rapidly from one of these comfort zones to the next in their
upriver migration in order to conserve energy. If steelhead are anything in a river,
they are creatures of water temperature and hydraulic comfort zones. Water temperature plays a big role in the type of hydraulics steelhead prefer and the closer
to the bottom end of the optimal temperature zone, the more benign the hydraulics they seek. Structure in the river creates hydraulic comfort zones for fish.

The Bottom and Edges

The bottom and the edges of a river create friction that slows water flow to .25 or
less of peak surface velocity ("1"). Less energy is required to swim upriver along
edges and bottoms and a lot less energy is required to hold there. The closer to the
bottom and edges our lures worked, the more effective we were. I cannot tell you
how many fish we hooked within 15 feet (or less) of the river bank. This comfort
zone is less than 20% of the total cross sectional area of a "hole". Therefore, we
tried to spend more time in the 20% of the water where fish were likely to be, instead of the 80% where they were not. This is the main reason we didn't waste time
fishing 20-foot depths since our lures would never get down to the fish. Why not
fish another way? We preferred our method and would just move to another spot
that had the water that suited how we wanted to fish—and did not waste time.

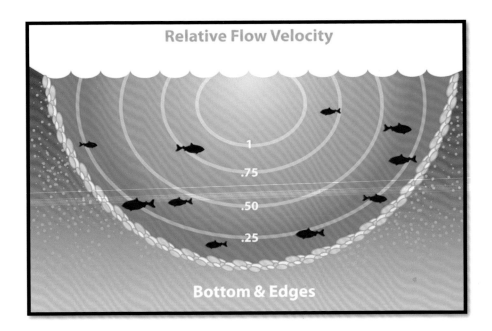

Boulders

Boulders create a tiny back eddy and hydraulic pockets that often hold fish. We can see some boulders sticking out above or just under the water's surface, but there are zillions of unseen larger rocks or boulders on the river bottom that create favorable hydraulics. We found the "pillow" in front of

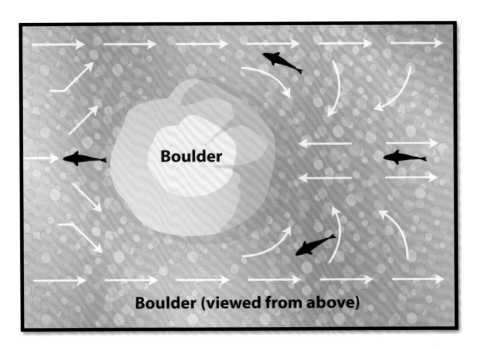

I see four spots a fish will hold here.

the boulder, the two seams at each edge of the turbulence behind it and the slower water where the flow came back together downstream from the boulder all had hydraulics that held fish.

Submerged boulders only differ in that they are three dimensional instead of two like the diagram and picture, and fish will also hold just above a submerged boulder in the uplift. Back-trolling lures is the most effective way to fish these spots because you can put a lure there and leave it there if you like. Other methods drift by and have to be recast. And lures usually do not snag or hang up on the structure like a drifted fly, spoon or jig can. Lures hold by them, bounce off them, around them and go by them at whatever speed you control with the boat.

Being surface dwellers, we have little choice but to reference a hook-up to a landmark on the river bank—a road sign, a tree, a building, an odd rock. I paid close attention to this when we would hook-up because 50-60 feet down river from that spot was something underwater I could not see that created the hydraulics that held a fish. When we would leave that spot, I tried to float over the top of it, look down and watch the depth finder to see if I could identify what it was. Most of the time, it was a boulder. Knowing where these little things are located really helps on the next trip down the river or when flows are higher or visibility is not as good.

Tailouts

Tailouts are just about everyone's favorite and I am no exception. The flow is rising up from a deeper place in the river creating a hydraulic "pillow" a migrating fish can rest upon. They use relatively little energy to stay in place. In addition, the fish has just moved quickly up through fast, relatively shallow current and generally stops to rest. The tailout is a deeper, safer place to rest in slower water. I believe steelhead stay in tailout hydraulics longer than in other hydraulic conditions. Carrying it one more step, the steeper and faster or longer and shallower the rapid or riffle, the better the fishing in the tailout above it.

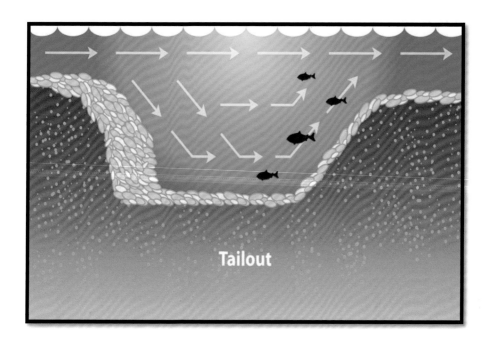

Tailout

As the water gets shallower in a tailout, it also picks up speed. The lures are diving deeper and closer to, if not bouncing off the bottom. Please notice again, the method produces "bouncing off" where other methods can "snag up on".

In warmer water, fish seemed to be at the bottom end of the tailout in the faster water. Often we would not hook-up until the lures were near the chute, just on the edge of where the water was starting to roll, beginning its descent down the rapid. Conversely, when water temperatures were cooler, the fish would be higher up in the slower water of a tailout.

Steelhead are not wired to swim back down a rapid after having made it up through fast water into a tailout. We have hooked a lot of steelhead even in the break of a tailout and rarely have had one take off down a rapid. If you hook one in a rapid they will usually take off downstream. But seldom will they leave a hole and go back down a rapid.

Classic tailout water.

Slots (Channels)

Slots (channels) run mostly parallel or at slight angles with river flow and the conjunction with bottoms and edges concentrate fish even more. In this instance let us assume we have a 100-yard-wide river and the slot is 20 yards wide. Fish are not going to be laying in two or three feet of still or slowly moving water—particularly on a sunny day. Steelhead will go find the slot. In this example

Slots and channels concentrate steelhead.

the slot is only 20% of the river surface area and fish are laying in the 20% of the slot on the "bottoms & edges". This means the comfort zone is less than four percent of the total river surface area. Therefore, we tried to fish the four percent of the water where fish were likely to be, instead of the 96% that was

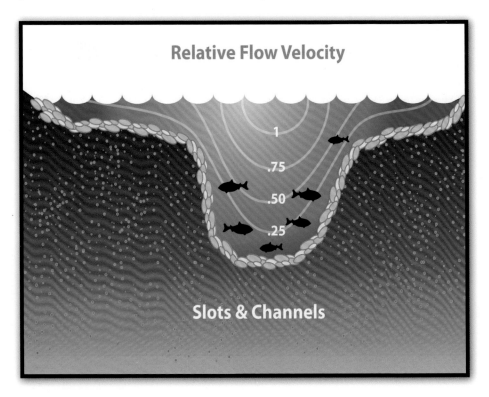

a long shot. The Clearwater has a lot of rather shallow, fast and flat bottomed water. Steelhead will make a beeline to the closest, deepest slot for safety and hydraulic comfort reasons. Even in a 2- or 3-foot-deep flat, a six-foot-deep slot will act like a fish magnet. And if the slot contains additional structure, you have all three working for you: the slot, bottoms and edges and boulders.

In extremely clear water, you can stand up and see these slots, but it is hard to row a drift boat standing up. My depth finder became part of me when fishing slots and was a much more efficient way to stay in productive water—particularly when the slots were in the middle of the river. You can see slots and channels much better from a higher vantage point, like the one in the picture, than from a boat seat. In a boat, move around and find them on the depth finder.

Ledges

Ledges are prevalent on the Clearwater River due to the basaltic nature of the rock formations. And you do not see them from a seat in a drift boat. These ledges rarely change as a result of their solid rock makeup. There are ledges that run at all angles to river flow and some even run perpendicular to flow but all drop almost straight down. These ledges provide cover for a steelhead, and shade at the right time of day. Plus, and maybe most important, they create hydraulics steelhead really like.

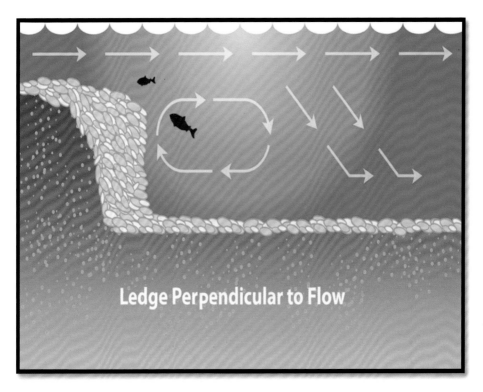

Ledge Perpendicular to Flow

A few perpendicular ledges come to mind right at the top of holes where a rapid dumps into the deeper part of a hole. Also, in the Lower River 3rd drift I mention in Chapter 14 there are two lava-rock points by the "ramp" where there are two ledges. The water drops from 5 to 10 feet then 20 yards down river drops from 10 to 15 feet. Fish hold on these ledges due to the hydraulics before continuing their journey. Once my depth finder read 15 feet, we would reel 'em up and either row back to the top in the frog water and go through again or go on down river to the next spot. It sure looks good and inviting to keep fishing on down through the hole, but back trolling lures that might be diving 10 feet deep in 15, 20, 25 feet of water we found was a waste of time and energy—low-probability fishing.

The two fish below came off these two ledges. We are at the rough take out and the ledges are under the chop behind us. Similar to the slot comments, I do not know how a person would find these ledges without a depth finder.

Another is a parallel ledge between the two highway side points in the hole above Lenore. I watched a wading fisherman find this ledge the hard way. A couple days later in the same stretch, I moved over to the area and saw on the depth finder the ledge the gentleman stepped off of, running between the points. From the fish log that day:

Living on the ledge (Gregg Larson right).

Comments: Hard to fish in afternoon with up-river wind and low flow. Last 4 fish came off two left points at Lenore that I'd never fished before.

The fish were between the points on the ledge. Next trip I found out there was a perpendicular ledge at the top of the first point. The next time I started higher in 2 feet of water so that the lures were diving off the ledge. This became an almost automatic two-hook-up spot for us and many times three or four. There are at least a dozen of these

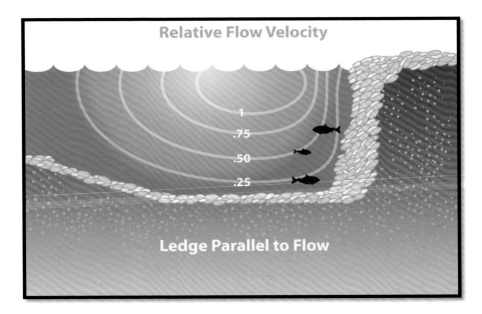

Relative Flow Velocity

1

.75

.50

.25

Ledge Parallel to Flow

in the 40 miles of river we fished and probably a dozen more we never had time to find. It is a combination of a ledge, an edge, a slot and points.

Points

Points create a lot of hydraulic changes in flow and are visible from above the surface. There is a hydraulic "lift" similar to a tailout right in front of a point

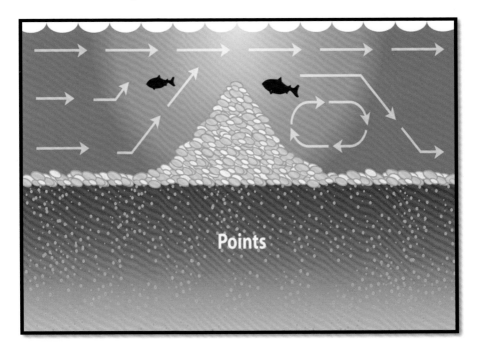

Points

Points are obvious and fishy.

and a depression behind it. We have hooked a lot of fish just above and just below points. Where you find points in tandem there is a depression between them that has reduced positive flow and usually a back eddy between them closer to the bank, creating a hydraulic seam along the edge that can also hold fish. So here you have tailout hydraulics, edges, a ledge affect, a seam and a bottom affect all working in your favor. Looking at tandem points I would see six places that were likely comfort zones to hold steelhead and would try to work the lures slowly in them all if possible. This is a very "snaggy" place to fish unless you are back-trolling lures that are bouncing off everything. Points and ledges are my favorite structures on the Clearwater River.

Back Eddys

Back eddys create hydraulic shear between main river flow and the back wash. This is a very narrow band of slower downriver flow that a migrating fish will hold in before zipping out and going on up the rapid or riffle—a seam. When I bank fished, I would stand at the top of the back eddy and short cast into the current allowing the spoon or drift bait to come back into the back eddy through this zone. Next cast would be a little further out coming back into the back eddy a little further down. I would visualize windows lined up side by side down this seam and try to bring the lure through a different window each cast from top to bottom. Once the spoon quit moving from the current, I would reel it in back through the backwash.

Contrary to popular opinion, steelhead avoid the backwash currents in a back eddy. They like water coming up from behind them into their gills about as much as we enjoy water coming out of our noses.

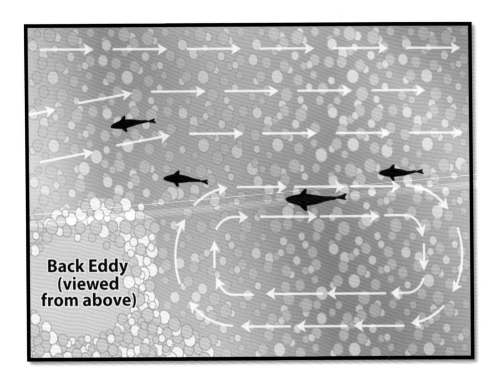

Back Eddy
(viewed
from above)

Yeah, I know. You caught a steelhead reeling back up through a back eddy. I'd bet a Red Hawg Boss you were reeling in either close to or in the seam and were attacked. Running a lure along these seams creates some tricky rowing. My fisherman helped with rod-tip movement to keep the lure in barely positive flow. Another technique is in the "comments" (page 109) from "Update October 21, 2011" at the end of Chapter 18 "Top 60 Days". Back-eddy seam hydraulics hold a lot of steelhead.

Runs

Runs do not need their own diagram. They are the straight lines and the 1 and .75 flow velocities **in the previous diagrams**. Runs are at the top of a hole and visible from the surface like **the photograph**. A steelhead's job is to get upstream to spawn. When the water temperature was in the higher end of optimal and fish were moving, they would hold in the tailouts to rest, scoot through slower water mid-hole areas and up to the top of a hole. This is the fastest water and again, only about 20% of the entire area. Steelhead pause in these fast-water spots before moving on. The very bottom of the tailouts and very top of the holes—the fastest water in a hole are the places fish will pause and bite. I could row around for hours in the easy-water middle, fishing and watching the rods wiggle and get a stray now and then but the fish were concentrated at the very top and very bottom of the holes. Put on your rowing shoes on these days.

Steelhead are real knuckle busters in runs like this.

Since steelhead are more comfortable in high 40's to low 50's water temperatures, they burn less energy and move the farthest and fastest. When they are moving, this is where they are concentrated and thus where your probabilities are highest. There are many days in September and early October when the water temperatures were in this range that runs were the only hydraulics in which we could hook fish.

I stood high above the river bank on an Alaskan river looking down into a very clear pool and watched some steelhead holding just under and a little down from the quick riffle entering the top of the pool. They were in an arrow-shaped group. Occasionally, the front fish would peel off and go to the back and a different one would become "point man". It was apparent to me that these fish were creating their own hydraulics.

It is most important to remember that:

Structures create hydraulics that pause upriver movement of migrating fish.
What type of hydraulics they favor is temperature dependent.
Flow fluctuations change the hydraulics of all structures.

When flows fluctuate, the hydraulic changes move the fish around. This is one reason why some days they are not necessarily where they were "yesterday". We could use our method in a variety of conditions. We learned that if one type of water didn't work for the conditions to quickly move and fish other types of water. I would think: "What do they like today?"

Very early on, I would wonder why my buddy hooked 5 one day and I hooked one or two. He hit on a set of hydraulic conditions that worked and kept doing it. I never hit on that condition . . . and kept doing it.

Insanity: "Doing the same thing over
and over again and expecting a different result."

—Albert Einstein

"Insanity" is much too strong a word in our context but this definition is the main reason 90% of steelhead fishermen catch only 10% of the steelhead. Ninety percent do the same thing every trip to the river, fishing the same way in the same place or same type water. Then when the conditions finally line up with their method, "the fish were biting that day".

Chapter 8

Flow

*F*low is a much bigger issue for fishermen than it is for fish; a much bigger issue for boat fishermen than bank anglers and a much bigger issue for drift boaters than power boaters. Higher and rising flow moves fish around, primarily upriver. Falling or lower flow slows this upstream movement.

In sorting through my data, we drew El Skunko 27 times in 309 days of fishing. Twelve (or 44%) of these fishless days were when the river was rising or had just finished rising and was still very high. When I sorted through the 60 best days we had, only six (10%) were in rising water conditions. And those six days were generally upriver, late-season, cold-water, low-flow times, just after the river got blasted with a warm, wet storm.

In another instance in the lower river we were in a spot that usually produces a fish or two. We hooked one, rowed over to shore, landed and released the fish. When I rowed back out, I could tell it required much more effort to stay in position. The river was rising or I was having a heart problem. I let it go and moved on down river but much faster than normal. I usually spent 45 minutes there but could only hold for about 15 minutes until my arms were in square knots. I floated down to another spot and noticed there was current at least 50 yards higher in the slot than normal. We never hooked another fish. In the last two really good holes we noticed the current was slowing back down. We fished them hard and never got a touch. Upon returning to my room, I called Dworshak Dam and asked what was going on. They told me they had raised flows from the dam from 1,500 CFS to 10,000 CFS for a couple hours to float a jet boat off the rocks in the McGill rapid.

El Skunko's

In the listing of all 27 of our El Skunko's, my ESE's (El Skunko Excuses) are highlighted! Sixty percent were flow related. Excuse some of the "generic" flow volumes listed above. Until real-time flow information was accessible on the web, we would gauge flow by how high the water was on "OK Rock".

You think I'm kidding, look to the left at water's edge as you cross the bridge into Orofino.

An obvious question would be that if we knew the conditions made the odds low of hooking a fish, why did we go anyway? Well, mostly I did not. But when friends and relatives come from out of town to fish—you go fishing.

El Skunko's

# Fish	Sky	Air Temp	Wind	Rising Falling	Visibility	H2O Temp	Flow
0	Cloudy		Breezy	Rising	Excellent	45	Steady - rising
0	Rain	42	None	Rising	Good	44	Rising
0	Cloudy	40	0	Steady		47	800 from Dam
0	Clear	38	Still	Steady	Very Clear	36	Average
0	Clear	41		Mod.High	Clear	38	4400
0	Clear	85	None	High	Clear	58	11,000 CFS
0	Clear	85	Still		Clear	62	1200 CFS low
0		51	Still	Steady	Good	45	4000 @ Peck
0	Clear	52	5	Rising	Very poor	49	6000 & rising
0	Rain	45	Still	High	Good	42	6800 @ Peck
0	Cloudy	45	Still	High	OK	41	6800 @ Peck
0	Cloudy	50	Breezy	Low	Extra Clear	48	3000
0	Clear	15	None	Steady	Very Clear	33	Very low
0	Clear	38	Still	High Steady	Clear	47	1200 CFS
0	Snow	32	15-25	Low/Falling	Very Clear	38	Very, very low,
0	Clear	60	0		Very Clear	52	Very low
0	Clear	55	0	Steady	Very Clear	41	3500 @ Peck
0	Clear		0				Very low & clear
0	Clear	72	0	High Steady	Very Clear	57	1700 CFS
0	Rain	40	Breezy	Low	Very Clear	41	3200
0	Clear	63	20-25	Varying	Fine	49	4800 - 5800
0	Clear	72	Calm	High	Clear	46	4700 @ Peck
0	Clear	60	Still	Rising	Very clear	50	1500 @ Orofino
0	Rain	50		Rising	5' Fairly Clear	48	3500 rising
0	Clear			Rising			6300 @ Orofino
0	Clear	60	15	Rising	2' Stained	46	5 to 6000
0	Clear	75	None		Vis 6'	53	3000

High-Flow Attitude

A gentleman I was doing some work for and his wife take an annual fishing trip somewhere in the world to get a picture of their catch to use on their Christmas card. They decided to come to the Clearwater from Cleveland, Ohio for a steelhead photo. I ask them to visit in October but November 7 (1991) was all that could be arranged. Of course it started raining and did not stop until mid day November 6. The river had risen to 5000+ CFS and visibility was 3 feet. This is not good. I lit incense, got out the finger symbols, sat on the floor, and summoned the positive mental attitude spirits. The places we had been hooking fish were much too fast at these flows to hold fish at this water temperature. I decided to fish the right hydraulics for the water temperature regardless of whether I had ever fished in the spot. We hooked 4 fish in places I had never fished and have not fished since and finally landed the last one. My friend Mickey called it "The Fish from Heaven" as only one other fish was hooked by our group's four boats.

Throwing out "Special Situations" and 13- & 18-fish days, the 60 best full days we had averaging 46 boat minutes per fish were when the water temperatures were optimal and the flows were as follows.

60 Best Days – River Stretch	Flow Range CFS	% Of Days River Rising, Steady or Falling
Upper River (32 Days)	2,500-3,900	90% Steady or Falling
Lower River (28 Days)	2,800-4,000	93% Steady or Falling

The question remains in my mind: is this when the fishing was best, or the flow where my ability and method combined to work best? I decided it is probably the latter but it doesn't really matter, this is how I wanted to fish and that is what this book is about.

Upper River Flow Comments: I noted in the log sheets that 2,500-3,200 was "perfect". For the table above I threw out a 13 fish day when flow was 2,340. I also noted that much below 1400, there was "not enough current to work the lures everywhere I wanted to fish them" and "I banged a lot of rocks." There is a note on a day when the flow was 890: "Don't do this again." It was easy to row and we caught some fish at 1,900 CFS. We also had some nice days at 3400-3900 when the river was falling but it's quite a bit quicker. If the water temperature was right, we did not hesitate to fish upriver if the flows were anywhere between 1,900-3,900 CFS.

Lower River Flow Comments: I don't how much value I will be in this category. I noted in the log sheets that 3200 was "optimal". Be ye advised that means it is optimal for ME—rowing a drift boat. Dworshak Dam's relatively stable discharge dampens to some degree the natural upper-river flow fluctuations. We had a lot of good days downriver in flows from 2,900-4,000 but that's a flow I could fish well—not necessarily THE optimal fishing flow. The river also gets wider the further it flows down toward Lewiston. Some of those great September days way down the river from Upper

Hog Island to Steelhead Park were in flows of 12,000 and I could still row the boat. Rowing 12,000 CFS at Peck would have put me in the hospital. I noted on one day when flow was 5000 that it was difficult. Power boats and bank anglers can fish much higher water than I can and I'm sure they do well in higher downriver flows than I am able to fish.

We usually don't fish with our pants around our ankles unless the steelhead utilize Trick #6 (see page 128).

Just for informational purposes, pages 65 and 66 show the 21-year average flows by month at Orofino and at Peck.

At Orofino, flows naturally rise from September through November as precipitation increases. Peck flows combine Orofino flows plus Dworshak Dam discharge. You can see the effects of the annual Dworshak dump in September at Peck.

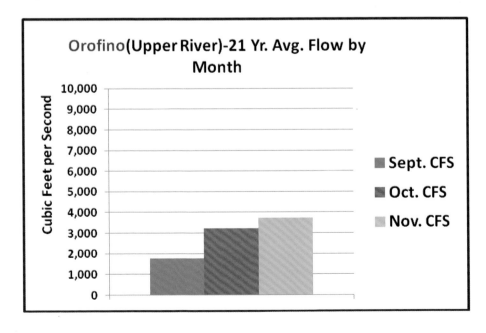

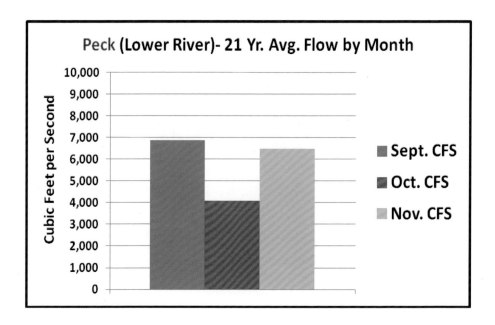

Water Clarity

Water clarity is occasionally an issue on the Clearwater. Mostly this happens when a big storm blows the river out. In this case flows alone generally kept us off the river. A few times when it had risen a lot and was falling we used "2 feet of visibility" as sort of a line in the sand. Almost every daily sheet I filled out has visibility at 6'-10' (Another statistic I kept that was of little use.) Occasionally, the South Fork Clearwater would "muddy up" after a good rain. This condition would add some color to the upper river but it was not really a huge problem. If there was any question, we would simply fish down river as the water discharging from Dworshak was as clear as a bell, diluting the more turbid flow from upriver. In a real pinch like an overnight downpour that blew the whole system out (with out-of-state relatives in town), we would go fish the mile of North Fork below Dworshak Dam as the 50-degree water coming from the bottom of the dam was never muddy. A couple times we went up above the mouth of the South Fork and fished the water above Kooskia and found good water conditions as well.

Partially documented, mostly opinion

When the river is rising, the music starts and it's time to boogie for a Slimerocket. They are not territorial anymore and could care less what you present to them unless you hit them right on the nose. When the music stops, it seems like it only takes a short time for them all to find a chair, get comfortable and begin defending their position.

I have not done well when steelhead were rolling all over the place in high or rising flow. I believe this is a sign fish are moving. However, if a fish rolls right behind your lures, stay put as you are irritating somebody.

To sum it up: Conditions!

I kept track of "Other Reports" in the log every day. John Kelly and Mike Smith were driftboat guides on the river during much of my record-keeping period. We generally talked each night to see how everybody did and where they would be fishing the next day. We wanted to make sure we were not leap-frogging each other down the same stretch of river the next day—them with paying customers and me just having a good time. Their results were virtually the same, if not better, every day if we fished the same section of the river—upper or lower. It was amazing how many days, fishing different drifts, we would all start hooking fish about the same time of day. Which drift was fished made little difference. When one of us would fish a different section of river the results varied. In other words when we fished similar conditions, the results were similar. The guy that fished a different section (condition) had a different result—better or worse—almost every time.

Chapter 9

Methods and "The Method"

*T*he data in this book is based on back-trolling lures as I mentioned at the beginning.

The first steelhead I ever caught was on a clown-colored Spin-N-Glo that I swear came right out from under the rock I was standing on as I was watching it and about to lift it from the water (the edge). It almost scared me to death.

The largest steelhead I ever landed was on a 7/8-oz. Pixie Spoon cast up into a rapid and allowed to settle down over the ledge in really fast water at the top of a hole.

The most incredible steelhead fishing I had was on a rather shallow Alaskan river (below), casting a #4 Vibrax spinner into a slot by an undercut bank. Virtually every cast was a hook-up—a dozen or more in three hours.

One of a dozen Alaskan steelhead on spinners.

Another Alaskan trip produced a couple nice steelhead while fly-fishing an Egg Sucking Leech in runs.

Until the Clearwater River, every steelhead I caught in colder water was drift-fishing corkies, etc., (the bottom) while casting from my drift boat or from the river bank, mostly in tailouts.

The edge, the ledge, the slot, the run, the bottom, the tailout—if you fish these places in the right conditions, it does not matter how you do it. What matters are where the conditions and hydraulics put the fish—then fishing that kind of water.

For me, the darned things are hard enough to hook-up to just crank in on heavy saltwater gear in a couple minutes. This is why we went to fly rods and single-action reels...the almost infinite drag of a palmed single-action reel allows for longer runs and more jumps (Slimerocket qualifications). And steelhead attack a back-trolled diving lure with shrimp consistently better than anything I have used. Drift boats are the easiest, second quietest way to access spooky, 36-inch trout, in small pockets of very clear water, on both sides of a six-mile stretch of rocky river. So we combined these three perversions into one, paid attention and hooked a lot of steelhead.

"The Method"

October 23, 1989, Mike Smith had fished about a mile down a drift with no action. He had seen several steelhead roll. He moved down the river to the next spot and but still no hook-up. Mike anchored, put on a larger lure and stuck a shrimp on the hook, put it out and immediately hooked up. He kept fishing that way the remainder of the day and hooked more fish than any of us that day. I began fishing this way the next day.

In my log of data, I took the 15 days (80 hours) we fished on the Clearwater prior to using Mike's method. I then looked up the next 80 hours we fished using Mike's method.

	Boat Hours Fished	Fish Hooked	Boat Hours Per Fish	*Rod Hours Per Fish (Boat X 2.5)
Lures alone	**80**	**41**	**1.95**	**4.87**
Lures with Shrimp	**82**	**55**	**1.49**	**3.72**

The "with shrimp" **data in the table** obviously was later in the season and there were more fish in the river during that time period. But there was also an average water temperature difference of 1.5 degrees (avg. 47.6 to 46.1) which should have made the fish a little more aggressive during the "lures

Steelhead performing trick #13.

alone" period. LOTS of variables, but I think it's safe to say we had 10%-20% more hook-ups with shrimp tails on the lures than without in optimal water temperatures. That is an extra fish per day.

I do not have the data to prove it as from that time on for the next 15 years we used shrimp. But my opinion is we got a lot higher than 10%-20% more hook-ups using shrimp when water temperatures were in the low 40's than without. Is it worth the hassle? You decide.

This is certainly not revolutionary, as this method and variations of it have been used for decades. But from this point forward we used shrimp tails and the vast majority of my data is based on this method.

Idaho law requires barbless hooks to facilitate easy release of wild and natural fish. Even still, trying to extract a barbless treble hook from a wild steelhead prior to release could be tedious and sometimes required netting and boating the fish. So we changed to single hooks and pinched down the barb. All hook-up data is based upon our method of fishing—back-trolling lures, with a shrimp tail on a single barbless hook from a drift boat.

Chapter 10

The Lures, the Best Colors

The Lures

*I*n the early years 1988-1989, we used mostly #35 "Hot Shots" made by Luhr Jensen. They rattled, worked great in fast water and ran true.

You have to use a snap on the eye for them to work best. Only issue I ever had with them was when the big fish arrived we would break one off every now and then because the lures are small and a big fish would get the whole thing in their mouth and the line would break on their teeth.

In the early 90's we added Hot-N-Tots by Storm as they

#35 Hot Shots.

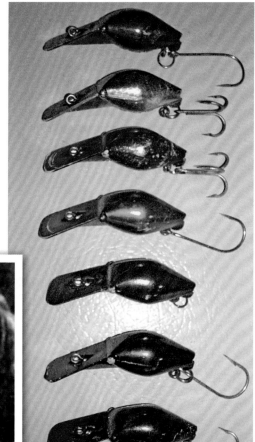

A real old Hot-N-Tot (the red one).

ran deeper and would still work when we started using shrimp where the #35 did not.

The only issue with these was the snap that came installed from the factory. We had 5 or 6 of them pull apart with a big fish on so we started taking the factory snap off and installing our own (pictured on the Rattle Tot below).

Then Storm came out with the Rattle Tot which was smaller than the Hot-N-Tot and had a bent-down lip where the Hot-N-Tot lip was straight.

It rattled and worked with bait. Again, we replaced the snap and treble hooks with our own and threaded it through the two top holes as you can

Rattle Tots, factory rig at top, our rig at bottom.

see in the photo to the left. It would dive deeper and work better in slower water.

This was my favorite until they quit making them. This little lure seemed to be a great combination of smallness, deep diving and a small shrimp tail on the hook did not affect the action. I tried to have one of these lures in the water most of the time.

In the mid 90's we added the Hawg Boss Super Toad by Yakima Bait Company (the model that floats). It would dive deeper and work better in really slow water. The Hawg Boss comes in a huge number of colors and was readily available so this became our mainstay. Each one comes with a black heavy-duty, factory-supplied snap (not pictured).

We still had to remove the trebles and put our single-hook rig on to use with shrimp. Usually, these things work great out of the box but occasionally one will have to be tuned which is simple. Just to show how these big B's test tackle, we had a batch of Black Hawg Bosses one year that had a lip defect we couldn't see. We would get a violent hit, set the hook and think we broke off or lost the fish and would come back with nothing but the black lip of the lure on the snap. Mike and I had a collection of five black lips! Hawg Boss graciously replaced them with new black lures which never came apart again.

Hawg Boss later came up with a couple of new striped colors that were really good. I liked the red one with the black stripes better than the plain red. They were sort of hard to find at times so I

Above: Our favorite Rattle Tot colors

Below: The Hawg Boss.

Clearwater steelhead like red.

Photo by Katherine Kelly

Top, Red Jail Bait, bottom, Jail Bait.

resorted to buying the solid colors and a black or red Sharpie pen.

Brad's Magnum Wigglers worked great early in the year in the warmer faster water. The little silver/orange one on the bottom right caught so many steelhead his eyes glazed over...

The Magnum Wiggle Wart was another excellent lure almost identical to the Brad's line (or vice versa). We used them with success and, as a matter of fact, had one of our top 6 days with these lures. That day I fished everything else I knew and all they would hit was Stu Kestner's Magnum Wiggle Wart.

It seemed however that in slower water, The Hawg Bosses or Rattle Tots were best.

Our Best Colors

It is a proven, documented fact that 100% of the fish we hooked were on the colors we were fishing with. You can quote me on that. So trying to be data-based on this subject may be misleading but I will give it a shot.

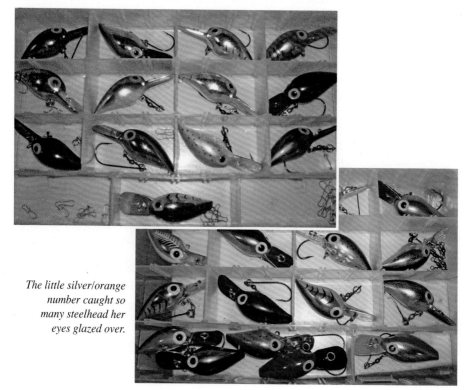
The little silver/orange number caught so many steelhead her eyes glazed over.

I can tell you we tried every color made. It's pretty obvious from the lure photos which were our favorites. They are all floaters, all have rattles, all work well in good current but the Hawg Boss Super Toad seemed to work best in slow-moving water as well. The Hawg Boss, Brad's and Wiggle Wart have the "widest" action and seem to dive deeper. The Rattle Tot has a tighter action and the #35 Hot Shot the tightest.

We switched around. And unless one color was all that made the fish angry that day, we usually had on two or three different colors. I liked to have at least one different brand of lure out too. We had a few of our own names for the multi-colored lures too, making it easier to communicate.

We followed the old saw—bright days bright colors, dark days dark colors—pretty closely. Green seemed to do well in both light conditions so seldom were the lures out working that at least one of them didn't have some green on it.

Bright days: in order of priority	Dark Days: In order of priority
Red	Purple
Metallic Pink (May West)	Black
Red/Silver/Blue (Miss America)	Green
Green	Blue
Silver/Orange Bars (Brad)	Red (if we got desperate)

Like other fish, some days steelhead would only hit one color regardless of what else we put in front of them. We would move the successful color around and that would be the rod that hooked up. We would even put on a different brand of the same color and that lure would hook-up.

I sorted the fish-on data by color. And I think **the list below** closely resembles the colors we fished most! Imagine that!

Below are the totals from my data of the number of fish hooked on each color.

Color (my description)	Number of Steelhead Hooked
Metallic Red	**192**
Metallic Green	**166**
Silver/Red/Blue	**158**
Metallic Purple	**152**
Metallic Pink	**137**
Glossy Black	**127**
Metallic Blue	**74**
Green/Gold/Red Pirate	**50**
Miscellaneous	**111**
Total	**1,167**

Single-action reels and fly rods are more fun.

I would bet that had I kept any data on how long we fished these colors, it would probably correlate closely if not exactly. In tabulating this I glanced at the light conditions (clear, cloudy or partly cloudy) and it lines right up with the "bright days, bright colors, dark days, dark colors" I mentioned above. But let me re-emphasize. It lines up because that's what we fished with.

I kept "fish hooked by lure records" in the logs. But they are of little benefit as they line up with what we fished with mostly in those years. That is 35 Hot Shots early on, Hot-N-Tots then Rattle Tots, Warts, Brad's and Hawg Bosses about the last half of the years recorded because they worked in all water.

On many occasions we would fish through a hole and if unsuccessful would row over to the back eddy and row back up to the top. We would change colors or brand or both and go back through it again. Often we would get a hook-up. I have no idea why this would work, but it did.

We tried all the magical, wonderful, mystery scents on the market. I cannot give you a "with scent vs. without" number because almost every entry after 1990 is "with". About half way through the time I collected data, we stuck on one that was available in a local tackle shop called Pop's Secret. I really cannot tell you why except that it was available and it sprayed on easily. It smelled like varnish to me. But after spraying the stuff on and hooking a steelhead, just try to put a fisherman's lure back in the water without it. I do not know what, if any, contribution this stuff made to our success, but I do know it did not hurt anything.

The barbs on the hook point must be bent down. The bait-keeper barbs on the hook shanks are legal and keep the shrimp tail from sliding down on the bend in the hook which stops the action of the lure.

Obviously, a single barbless hook makes getting a steelhead to the boat more of a challenge, particularly a "hot" Slimerocket. We brought an average

76   STRIKING STEELHEAD

of 60.3% of the steelhead we hooked to the boat using level-wind reels. That fell to almost 50% with fly rods and single-action reels as they were harder to hook and there were more runs and jumps. We used level-wind reels with 8'-9' rods or fly reels with 7-9-weight fly rods. We used 12-14-pound monofilament line and found anything much heavier than 14-pound line effected the action of the lures in slower current. We tried copolymer monos and braided low-stretch lines and these broke repeatedly upon the shock of a violent hit.

Undocumented opinion

I think the stretch of standard monofilament was needed as a shock absorber, particularly in faster current with the line tests we used.

We had the most fun with fly rods and fly reels loaded with monofilament (yes, to back-troll lures). We would get the same number of hook-ups but a lot more jumps (and busted knuckles). It's good for the reel parts business also!

Lures were fed out in the current and fished 50-60 feet downriver from the front of the boat which I held steady in the current with the oars. I almost always had two fishermen in the front of my drift boat and about half the time put my rod out while doing the boating. Distance out was not as critical as both front fishermen being out the same distance.

Since I usually rowed the boat, I always fished mine "short" 30 to 40 feet out the left side. This spread the two long lures out better and helped to avoid the tangle "noid" when we got a fish on. This also gave me a little extra time to handle the boat, oars and anchor until I could get my line out of the way.

All my data is in boat hours. In fast current or when fishing got hot I would put my rod away. Occasionally, I would have one passenger and, not enough times, went alone. I figure my set-up was in the water maybe half the time I was in the boat. So I arbitrarily and conservatively picked 2.5 as the number of rods fishing at any given time. It was probably less. So if hours-per-rod is of interest to you, just multiply the boat figure by 2.5.

Chapter 11

Time of Day

I was standing at the fish-counting window at McNary Dam one day watching steelhead swim past the window on the other side of the wall from where the fish counters were working. One of the fish counters walked out to go on break. I asked this person what time of day they saw the most activity. In other words, what time of the day are these fish most inclined to tackle a fish ladder? I was told that from 10 a.m. to 2 p.m. there was more movement and more fish counted. Interesting.

I sorted my data for what time of day we hooked fish to see what the data said. Much like the comment on colors, "100% of the fish we hooked were when we were on the river with lures in the water."

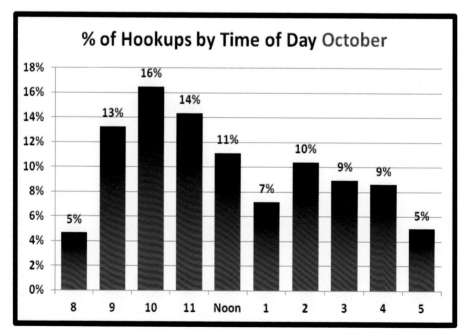

"9" would be fish we hooked between 9:00-10:00 a.m. etc.

Several things are interesting to me:

- First, the best three hours of the day are 9:00 a.m. to Noon regardless of which month. We hooked 42.5% of our fish in these three hours of the day.
- Second, we hooked a higher percentage of our daily totals on November afternoons than on October afternoons which probably speaks to the cold-water warming I mentioned earlier.
- Third, there was not much fishing after 4:00 pm in November due to Daylight Savings Time but we went out earlier. This is completely contrary to what I had thought.
- Fourth, you can see we anchored-up (with lures out) to eat lunch around noon to 1:00 p.m., or the fish were moving like the fish-counter's comment would suggest.

If I sort the data in three-hour periods to keep it simpler from start to 11 a.m., 11 a.m.-2 p.m. and 2 p.m. until the end of the day, it looks like this:

Start until 11:00 a.m.	11:00 a.m. – 2:00 p.m.	2:00 p.m. until end of day
37%	31%	32%

I was really surprised by this. I had always liked the first two and last two hours of the day and thought the differences would have been more dramatic.

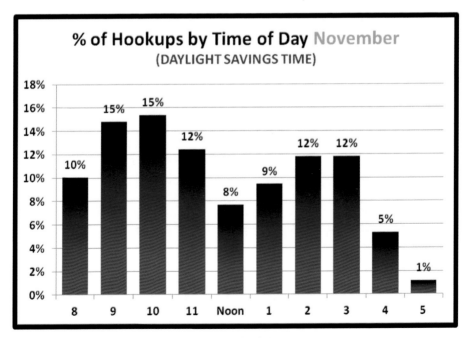

"9" would be fish we hooked between 9:00-10:00 a.m. etc.

There are a couple other things here that I think are noteworthy:

First of all, there is almost a three-hour difference in the number of hours of daylight from the first of October to the end of November. So the October data has more full three-hour periods early and late. Second, November, by contrast, has few full late-day periods because we would have been fishing in the dark due to Daylight Savings Time. Cleaning steelhead in ice water while holding a flashlight in your teeth is tricky. As a result, both months have full mid-day periods reflected in the data. But there were very few full late-day periods in November.

Undocumented opinion

Considering the fish-counter's comments that steelhead move more during mid day and my memory of morning and evening fishing, I think in the late afternoon, early-evening, steelhead slow down and are settling in for the night and once settled, defend their comfort spots. For the most part they are still in these spots in the morning and are more aggressive. Several of my fishing friends live for fishing the last hour of daylight.

Fly-fishermen seem to come out of the woodwork in the evenings too, for good reason. There is reduced fishing pressure, there is shade on the water and fish are settling into holding spots. And since, genetically, fly-fishermen have to stand in the water they run a lower risk of being run over by a power boat! They do it the hard way in September and October wading out to within cast-able distance of runs, slots and tailouts. The last hour of daylight, they are standing in the river while the rest of us are already in toasting the fish gods. We had a special name for this time of day on the Clearwater...

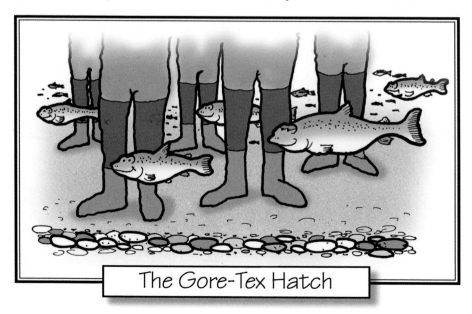

The Gore-Tex Hatch

I have been towed down a few rocky, river banks in low light by a big "B". I think that is why they put knee pads on Gore-Tex waders.

Fishing after dark is not something done often in a drift boat as going down the Clearwater River in the dark is not very bright. However, I was forced into doing this twice at gunpoint—both times after a relatively slow, full-day drift.

October 19, 1991, Chris Oakes and Tom Myers conned me into putting in, fishing and taking out in the same hole. So we did and hooked eight steelhead in two hours. First time I ever "listened" for a jump. Unhooking and releasing a thrashing steelhead in the dark with a flashlight in your teeth takes talent.

October 2011
Orofino, Idaho (approximate time any year)

Sunday	Monday	Tuesday	Wednesday	Thursday	Friday	Saturday
						1 Sunrise: 6:43am Sunset: 6:27pm
2 Sunrise: 6:44am Sunset: 6:25pm	3 Sunrise: 6:45am Sunset: 6:23pm	◑4 Sunrise: 6:47am Sunset: 6:21pm	5 Sunrise: 6:48am Sunset: 6:20pm	6 Sunrise: 6:49am Sunset: 6:18pm	7 Sunrise: 6:51am Sunset: 6:16pm	8 Sunrise: 6:52am Sunset: 6:14pm
9 Sunrise: 6:53am Sunset: 6:12pm	10 Sunrise: 6:55am Sunset: 6:10pm	11 Sunrise: 6:56am Sunset: 6:08pm	○12 Sunrise: 6:57am Sunset: 6:06pm	13 Sunrise: 6:59am Sunset: 6:04pm	14 Sunrise: 7:00am Sunset: 6:02pm	15 Sunrise: 7:01am Sunset: 6:01pm
16 Sunrise: 7:03am Sunset: 5:59pm	17 Sunrise: 7:04am Sunset: 5:57pm	18 Sunrise: 7:06am Sunset: 5:55pm	19 Sunrise: 7:07am Sunset: 5:53pm	◐20 Sunrise: 7:08am Sunset: 5:52pm	21 Sunrise: 7:10am Sunset: 5:50pm	22 Sunrise: 7:11am Sunset: 5:48pm
23 Sunrise: 7:13am Sunset: 5:46pm	24 Sunrise: 7:14am Sunset: 5:45pm	25 Sunrise: 7:15am Sunset: 5:43pm	26 Sunrise: 7:17am Sunset: 5:41pm	●27 Sunrise: 7:18am Sunset: 5:40pm	28 Sunrise: 7:20am Sunset: 5:38pm	29 Sunrise: 7:21am Sunset: 5:36pm
30 Sunrise: 7:23am Sunset: 5:35pm	31 Sunrise: 7:24am Sunset: 5:33pm					

November 2011
Orofino, Idaho (approximate time any year)

Sunday	Monday	Tuesday	Wednesday	Thursday	Friday	Saturday
		1 Sunrise: 7:26am Sunset: 5:32pm	2 ◑ 3 Sunrise: 7:27am Sunset: 5:30pm First Qtr: 8:39am	3 Sunrise: 7:28am Sunset: 5:29pm	4 Sunrise: 7:30am Sunset: 5:27pm	5 Sunrise: 7:31am Sunset: 5:26pm
DST Ends 6 Sunrise: 6:33am Sunset: 4:25pm	7 Sunrise: 6:34am Sunset: 4:23pm	8 Sunrise: 6:36am Sunset: 4:22pm	9 Sunrise: 6:37am Sunset: 4:20pm	10 ○ 11 Sunrise: 6:39am Sunset: 4:19pm Full Moon: 12:17pm	11 Sunrise: 6:40am Sunset: 4:18pm	12 Sunrise: 6:42am Sunset: 4:17pm
13 Sunrise: 6:43am Sunset: 4:16pm	14 Sunrise: 6:44am Sunset: 4:14pm	15 Sunrise: 6:46am Sunset: 4:13pm	16 Sunrise: 6:47am Sunset: 4:12pm	17 Sunrise: 6:49am Sunset: 4:11pm	18 ◐ 19 Sunrise: 6:50am Sunset: 4:10pm Last Qtr: 7:10am	19 Sunrise: 6:51am Sunset: 4:09pm
20 Sunrise: 6:53am Sunset: 4:08pm	21 Sunrise: 6:54am Sunset: 4:07pm	22 Sunrise: 6:56am Sunset: 4:06pm	23 Sunrise: 6:57am Sunset: 4:05pm	24 ● Sunrise: 6:58am Sunset: 4:05pm New Moon: 10:11pm	25 Sunrise: 7:00am Sunset: 4:04pm	26 Sunrise: 7:01am Sunset: 4:03pm
27 Sunrise: 7:02am Sunset: 4:03pm	28 Sunrise: 7:04am Sunset: 4:02pm	29 Sunrise: 7:05am Sunset: 4:01pm	30 Sunrise: 7:06am Sunset: 4:01pm			

I told them they were all wild so I did not have to clean fish too. They figured that out during cocktail hour.

One 18-degree late-November evening my wife, Pam whined about keeping a couple fish because it was our last trip of the year. I found myself sliding the boat out over six feet of frozen river to the water. The water temperature was 33 degrees. She landed dueling 16-pounders in 30 minutes of fishing. It does not take long to land a frozen steelhead. John Kelly was nice enough to drive down to the river when he saw our truck lights and sit in front of the heater with Pam while I stood in a 33-degree river and cleaned two frozen steelhead on an ice shelf.

The best Clearwater fishing I ever had for steelhead was in the dark.

Chapter 12

Fishing Pressure, Weather Factors, Light

River Traffic and Fishing Pressure

*A*bout half of our time was spent in the lower river due to the conditions being more favorable that given day. We were as successful there as in the upper river. There is more boat traffic obviously because power boats fish this area and the water is bigger. I have noticed if there is a lot of traffic fish seem to be more concentrated on the edges of the river but I have no data to back that up. It may be because that's where we would fish in those situations.

I tried not to fish much in crowds due to our method. It is just plain rude to pull up and start fishing right in front of or right below a bank or wading fisherman. The same applies to pulling in right behind a power boat that is drifting or back-trolling. When there was a crowd and it seemed like every spot had someone in it, we would use that time to explore new spots, fish way above them, or quit. There are more places to fish than there is time to fish them. Life is too short to crowd other fishermen on a river. But river traffic (of all varieties) and fishing pressure affect results—the data is irrefutable.

October 15 - Opening Day

All but a short distance of the Clearwater at its mouth is catch and release only until October 15th. The rationale is twofold. First is to ensure escapement to the hatcheries for production purposes. The second is to spread fish up through the drainage to spread opportunity for fishermen. Sitting in restaurants in early October I have been asked countless times: "You're fishing? The season doesn't even open until the 15th." We have a name for "October 15th Opening Day" on the Clearwater…

The Aluminum Hatch

I kept which day of the week we fished in my records during the entire log period. I did not pay real close attention to this data at the time. I noticed which days of the week we chose to fish evolved from a couple days on the weekend to more mid-week days due to fishing pressure on the river. When I sorted the data, I was amazed at the difference in our hook-ups per hour on various days of the week. I even went back and double checked. Here is the data:

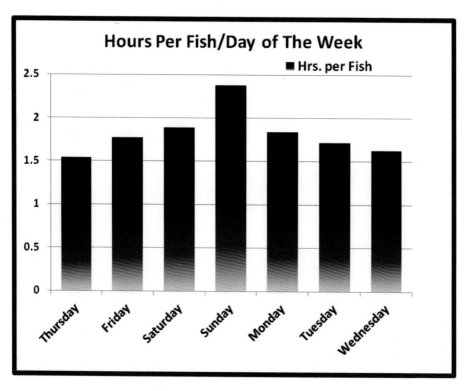

Believe it...the worst three days of the week to fish are Saturday, Sunday and Monday. Here is the data in table form:

Day of The Week	Hours per Fish
Sunday	2.38
Monday	1.84
Tuesday	1.72
Wednesday	1.63
Thursday	1.54
Friday	1.77
Saturday	1.89

This tells us that when all other things were equal, a seven-hour float would result in 4.54 hook-ups on a Thursday vs. 2.94 hook-ups on a Sunday. That looks like this:

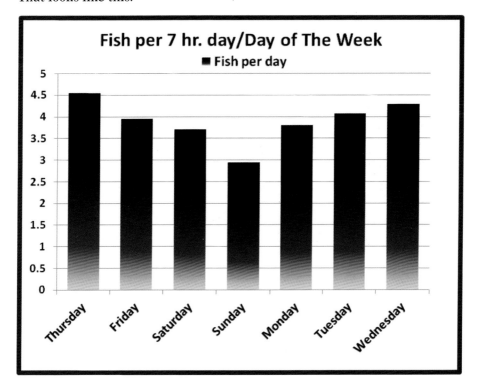

I double checked the data and threw out all the special situations in August, September and December to give me a true picture of average, full-day October-November fishing and the differences were even more dramatic. Fishing pressure? Biters are being removed? Fish are spooked? You decide.

Sun, Shade and Clouds
Steelhead do not have eyelids. That is science.

Undocumented opinion
I only kept records of general light conditions "clear, cloudy, partly cloudy, rain" etc. and not "light by fish hooked". As you know, this often changes throughout the day as well. The Clearwater has, well, very clear water and thus I think bright sun effects hook-up rates. This also can change from October to November. When the water is at the upper end of optimal, I looked for shade on the water or chop on the surface that refracted the light. By shade I mean from trees on the bank to broad shade cast by hills close to the river bank to the shady side of boulders. Chop being mostly at the top of a hole where the rapid enters. Slight breeze riffling the surface also seemed to help.

Rae Tway with a "bright day in the shade" steelhead.

One bright, warm, perfectly still early October day we had drawn El Skunko until noon. I decided to try shade even if it was in places I did not normally fish. We hooked 6 fish—all in shade the next five hours and two in places I had never fished.

On cloudy days of course this was not an issue—we liked cloudy days in the warmer water times in October.

November clouds were welcome as well until the water temperature dropped into the lower end of the optimal range. Then it seemed that bright bluebird days had the effect of warming the water a degree or two in the afternoon which seemed to trump the brightness and the fish would really turn on. This effect was most pronounced in the upper river where nature alone controlled the thermostat.

It also seemed that the angle of the light mattered. Most steelhead face upriver and our lures were approaching them from up river. With the sun at our back, it was shining directly into the fishes eyes. With the sun in our faces, it was at the steelheads back—and also illuminated the lures from a better angle for the fish to see them. As goofy as that sounds we seemed to do better. (Most steelhead face upriver—I did see a guy trolling upriver catch one once. We are talking the river part of the river here, not the Great Snake Lake part of the river.)

Wind

I only recorded wind if it was a problem—which it was some days. More than anything, it affected boat handling.

Undocumented opinion

Nobody likes wind on a river except fish. A little chop is one thing and it's helpful on bright days. But high wind makes rowing a drift boat like trying to row a kite. The lures are jerking around and less effective. Wind affects power boaters trying to drift fish as they go too fast or too slow, and bank anglers fight casting and wind effects on line, as well. I've talked to a lot of fishermen and it does not seem that anyone does well in high wind. The upper river is generally a little less windy than the lower river.

Extremely high wind is dangerous in a drift boat and it does not have to be a storm either. Twice we were almost blown over on a sunny day by gusts that came seemingly from nowhere.

Once I was sitting in the front of my boat while a friend took us down a rapid on the Salmon River with which I was unfamiliar. As we picked up speed entering the chute, a gust of wind hit us from the side, moved us about 20 feet right and we collided with an exposed boulder. We all saw it coming. I held on but still ended up going out of the front of the boat into the river. This happened twice that day. It never happened again nor did it ever happen on the Clearwater. If the wind gets extreme, row to the bank, pull the boat way up on the rocks and get off the river.

Rain

Only six of our "Top 60 Days" were in the rain. That means 54 were not in the rain. Usually rain comes with clouds which we liked. Of course the real issue with significant rain is the effect on flow and water temperature. If it rained hard, fishing was difficult perhaps because we were miserable and didn't fish as effectively.

You guys are all wet.

More than once we have had a trip altered by prolonged rain which blew the river completely out. We would simply go fish the North Fork below Dworshak Dam which flows clear 50-degree water regardless of the weather. It is a bit confining but we have caught a lot of fish in the North Fork on days like the picture...but it rains there too! Shortly after this picture was taken, the main river got so high, it backed up into the North Fork, reversed flow from downriver to upriver and raised water levels rapidly.

Barometric Pressure

I kept barometric pressure in generic form: High, Rising, Falling and Low. This was a bit subjective and easy when the weather was stable but impossible when weather was unstable with the barometric pressure jumping around all day.

Barometric Pressure	Hours per Hook-up
High	1.71
Rising	1.81
Falling	1.79
Low	1.74

Barometric pressures seem to affect fishing for species that are eating. But I could not determine that it made steelhead more or less grumpy or territorial or correlated with fishing results. I suppose it was worth collecting 18 years of data to know that the barometer really doesn't affect steelhead fishing much at all. Still it seemed like right before a storm fish would turn on.

Solunar Periods

I also kept Solunar period data for a couple years. Like the barometric pressure data, I found little correlation with our success on the Clearwater. Major and Minor Solunar periods may have a much bigger effect on coastal streams due to tide activity, but 500 miles inland I could not determine there was any affect so I quit recording it.

Steelhead spooks...and things that go "bump" in the river

It doesn't seem that steelhead spook very easily. But the data says otherwise. The overriding instinct of any critter is self preservation. Steelhead are no different. Don't blow this off. This is the reason they lay in a hole where they do—safety, energy preservation and oxygen. This is the reason you best move when you see a family of river otters playing in the hole you are fishing or a deer takes a swim in your spot just as you get there. This is the reason you will not see them lying in two feet of still water with eagles flying around. This is why you are wasting your time when you pull into a spot where kids on the bank have been chucking rocks in the river... or when a bank fisherman's dog swims out to retrieve your steelhead.

It is best to just move on to the next spot—the steelhead already have—I do not care how good the spot is.

On a particularly miserable cold, wet November day in the upper river, we had a friend in the boat that had never caught a steelhead and want-

Yes, that's Fido swimming out to "help" us net our fish.

ed one in the worst way. We were looking straight in the eye of El Skunko late in the afternoon (it never fails). But I knew we had a great chance of a hook-up in the last spot.

We floated down to it, all the way with me chattering about this being a great spot and our chances being good there. I pulled up, stopped the boat and dropped the anchor. The lures were put in the water and things were set.

I pulled the anchor and started to row when a young buck whitetail deer came trotting out of the bushes on the river bank and bails off into the river between the boat and our lures, hell bent for the other side of the river. I yelled (not smart) which did nothing but confuse the animal. Now he did not know which way to swim. I told my fishermen to hold their rod tips way up so we did not end up with a wad of monofilament and a couple of sharp Owner hooks in a swimming whitetail.

Down into the hole this cluster of confusion floated until the deer decided to swim back to the side of the river it came from. We reeled 'em up and floated down to the ramp.

Chapter 14

Ðrift Map

(I am not superstitious, there is just no chapter 13 in this book)

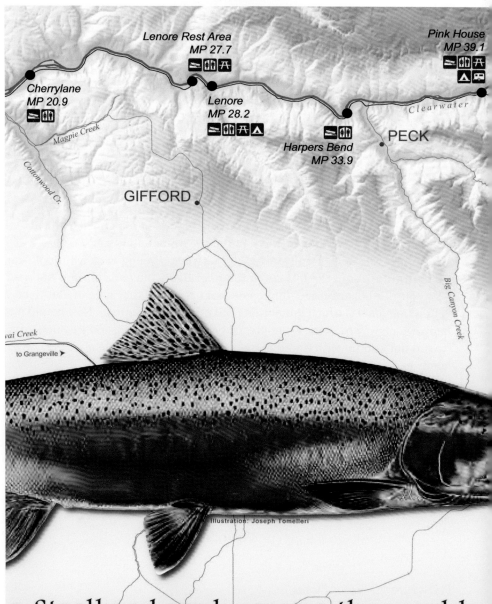

Cherrylane
MP 20.9

Lenore Rest Area
MP 27.7

Lenore
MP 28.2

Harpers Bend
MP 33.9

Pink House
MP 39.1

Clearwater

PECK

Magpie Creek

Cottonwood Cr.

GIFFORD

Big Canyon Creek

vai Creek

to Grangeville ▶

Illustration: Joseph Tomelleri

g Steelhead rank among the worlds

We did 99% of our fishing in the 46-mile stretch between Kamiah and Cherry Lane. **(See the map).** We stayed in Orofino which is in the middle of this 46-mile stretch and more convenient to access the stretches of river we wanted to fish in either direction. We fished some areas above and below this area but not enough to be of any statistical significance. That is the only reason they are not included in this book. Remember, in this book Ahsahka is the dividing line between upper and lower main sections. Water temperature and flow conditions determined whether we fished the upper or lower river and my data says we fished each about half of the time. All of these drifts have nice, concrete boat ramps at both put-in and take-out (except the airport and Lava Rock). All things being equal, we would fish the "no motors water"

Campgrou

Picnic Are

Restroom

North Fork Access
Ahsahka Access

ROFINO

Orofino Creek

12

Zans
MP 49.3

Jim Ford Creek

Location

IDAH(

Five Mile
MP 54.3

Lolo Creek

Sixmile Creek

Long Camp
MP 61

Kamiah City Par
MP 66.7

niere sportfish!

above Orofino. When I started, I concentrated on a few "spots" John and Mike showed me. Then as I got more familiar with the river and the drifts, I began to fish similar water both up and down the river.

It's almost as if the BLM had this book in mind when they published this map. The map includes improved boat ramps, a legend that lists additional facilities and includes names and distances between them all the way from Kooskia to Lewiston. You can find a larger version of this map on the web at: http://www.blm.gov/pgdata/etc/medialib/blm/id/rivers/clearwater.Par.0611. File.dat/Clearwater.pdf. Thank you, BLM.

Photo by Katherine Kelly

The "Grandma River"

From a drift-boater's perspective, a friend told me the Clearwater is a "Grandma river". To a Rogue River drift-boat guide or whitewater rafter this is true. There is nothing "technical" about the parts of the Clearwater we consistently fished during steelhead season. But there seems to be a place or two in every drift where you need to pay attention, know which way to go and know how to row a drift boat. The Clearwater is boney in low flow. A lot of this low flow is during steelhead season. Take some time and look it over before you drift it. Ask any of us who have fallen in. The learning curve is pretty steep in 45-degree water with hip boots, waders or heavy clothes on whether it is technical or not.

—*Signed, Grandma Dan*

Chapter 15

Upper River Favorite Drifts

"They are where you find them."

—John Kelly

he Clearwater River has a cobble-rock bottom almost throughout its length. There is very little sand or fine-gravel "structure" that shifts from blowout to blowout like in coastal rivers. However, from year to year, the spring thaw and accompanying high water can change the hydraulics in a hole. Not visually, necessarily, or even noticeably from a surface-flow perspective. Perhaps the annual spring flood moves a couple submerged boulders around a bit or moves and re-channels the cobble slightly on the river

"Clearwater Dreamtime"

Photo by Mike McElhatton www.digitalartsphotography.com

bottom. Something in the hydraulics can change a spot from being the hottest spot on the river one year to below average the next—or vice versa. We would fish places that in the past were poor and found great fishing—and vice versa. These subtle changes can also alter where steelhead will hold. Multiply this by changing water temperature and flow conditions which will move fish around and: "They are where you find them."

A couple examples:
Whenever Mike Smith, John Kelly and I would fish together, we'd take turns on the oars. We would get to a spot and start fishing whenever the rower said. Invariably the conversation would be:

"Why are we starting here?"
"Well, this is where I fish it, where do you fish it?"
"I start down there."
"I've never fished it that low." etc. etc.
Get my drift?

My son-in-law, Randy Dawson (the guy holding the fish on the cover) had fished with me a few times and one day brought his GPS to mark the holes we fished on a drift in the upper river. We had a nice day, hooked some fish and Randy marked all the places we fished. A few days later he took his own boat and did the same drift with some of his friends. He fished a couple places we had gone right over and did better than we had together. The following year I asked him if the GPS stuff was still working. He said the places were fairly obvious and he was not using it much. He did the same thing on a lower river drift, following me in his own boat. He fished places around us that he thought looked good on his depth finder, but not the same spots where we fished. Randy did almost as well—alone—as three of us combined did in my boat.

This is another reason that GPS coordinates are not of much benefit to identify "hot spots" from year to year. Many change from year to year and we obviously did not know them all that year anyway. We all have to find them every year. There are not many magical, wonderful, secret honey holes that produce every single year. You will know the few there are because there are people and boats all over them. Magical and wonderful maybe, but certainly not secret.

I fished holes and places in those holes that matched the conditions. This is the fun part for me. Figuring it out, watching a rod bury over the front of the boat and watching adults turned into children when a Slimerocket flies out of the water.

The Upper River is more "saucer shaped" structurally than the lower river, except the canyon portion. It is shallower overall than the lower river, has longer riffles, smaller holes and shorter slots, cuts or channels of deeper water. This topography seems to concentrate the fish more in fewer, smaller areas. This also provides for easier visual identification of holding areas. Following a big rise in river flows, this stretch can be fantastic after the river settles and falls back below 4000 CFS. We chose to fish the upper river whenever conditions were even close to right. In going through my data, which of these three upper river sections we chose was almost a coin toss. As you can see in the following chart, there wasn't much difference in fish hooked between these three drifts when the conditions were the same.

Abby Hayes' first trip and third fish, October 2000.

We made up our own names for the spots we fished that no one else would probably recognize, not to be secretive but so we could communicate without lengthy descriptions. The secret is they are not secrets. All are easily recognizable from the river and more so from the highway to anyone with even a small degree of water-reading ability. Rule of thumb was if it was 3-10 feet deep with current, fish it if you have time when the conditions are right.

With the above ingrained in the brain the following are the boat hours per fish we hooked, by drift in the upper river.

Upper River Drift	Average Boat Hours per Hook up
Kamiah to Long Camp	1.53
Five Mile to Zans	2.80
Zans to the Airport	1.22
Zans to Slaughterhouse	1.37

Don't take this as a 100% commentary on fishing being better in one drift than another. Travel time between holes is included in these averages. I recorded hours from "take-off to landing" and not the hours lures were in the water. The longer the drift and travel time between spots, the higher the hours per fish. I think the "Five Mile" number is high because it includes times we would beach the boat at Greer and walk up to the Greer Tavern for "lunch". Mike Smith owned the Greer Tavern at the time. But I didn't think we were there THAT long!

Kamiah to Long Camp: an old railroad bridge.

The first drift Kamiah to Long Camp = 5.7 miles (1.53 boat hours per hook-up). It is the "coolest" of the four since the majority of the lower few miles are shaded after noon. We put-in at the nice ramp at the Kamiah Bridge.

A slot by exposed boulders.

There are 22 different places we fish and have hooked fish in this drift—from the hole at the bridge where you put-in, to the hole just below the ramp where you take-out—again all plainly visible. The best places seem to be the slots and where there are rocks in the middle of the river, of course one should fish the deeper side. Stay in the slots, which is much easier with a depth finder for the person sitting in the rower's seat. My depth finder also had a temperature gauge—very handy. There are a couple longer holes so make sure you fish the points and boulders. There are larger boulders all over the bottom of this stretch unseen until you look down into the river, making back-trolling lures most effective. Take your time as it is not a long drift but make sure you do not over-shoot the ramp at Long Camp by much—it's seven miles through the canyon to the next one.

The canyon in the Long Camp to 5 Mile drift.

The second drift Long Camp to 5 Mile = 6.8 miles. We only did this once for three reasons. First, seven miles is a fair haul on a short November day. Second, there are a couple extra boney spots up high in the drift and one rapid at a bend that takes more than mediocre skill (that would be me) to safely pass in low water.

A boney spot.

Structure is easier to see from the road than the river.

Third, we had 40 other miles of river, 15 that were pleasantly uncrowded, so who needed this? They must be the same reasons most everyone else avoids it as well. We hardly ever saw a boat in this drift. The water, slots and structure look as good as, or better than, anything on the upper river and I am certain the fishing is comparable. Were I to move back to Idaho and have the time, I would probably concentrate on this area.

The third drift Five Mile to Zans = 5 miles (2.80 boat hours per hookup). This is a fun and pretty stretch of river. There are many places to fish—three or four in the first big hole. There are 18 places we have caught fish in this drift—four in the first hole and one upriver from the ramp. There are several different kinds of water on this drift. The water is a bit deeper and fish are scattered in most every hole from top to bottom. There is fast water, slow water, runs and chop. Like all drifts in the upper river, fish the slots of deeper water, boulders and the deep side of the rocks in the river. The points with current moving by them can be really good if flow conditions are right. In optimal water temperatures, rowing upstream from the ramp is good. Lolo Creek flows in at the bottom of the first hole. Leave time for the last two holes particularly the run right-center above the ramp at Zans. Hooking a big steelhead there and netting him at the ramp is a great way to end the day.

The fourth drift Zans to "The Airport" = 5.25 miles (1.22 boat hours per fish). I like this drift a lot. There are 21 places we have hooked fish in this drift. Obviously the holes are not long distances apart so you are fishing more, floating less—and the hours per fish show it. This drift gets away from the highway in several places. Like the 5 Mile Drift, in optimal water temperatures, rowing upstream from the ramp around the point as far as you can is a good spot. Looking down from the ramp, the first point on the left falls off into the type of slot you are looking for. Above Fords Creek can be good. Same deal as above—fish the deep side of boulders in the river and slots anywhere. The run just above the Orofino

Bridge is the last hole and once you go under the bridge the next stop is the take out at the Airport. I like this drift too because you have two options for take-out if there is a lot of pressure on the river. One of them, (right) is a crude, unpaved, unimproved, rock garden at the east end of the Orofino Airport. Do not try this one without four-wheel drive if the rocks are wet. The other is the fifth drift below.

The fifth drift is a quickie, Airport to Slaughterhouse (Ahsahka Access) = 2.1 miles or can be added on to the Zans drift making it 7.35 miles. This little drift starts at the airport "ramp" (right) and goes behind the airport.

The airport "ramp".

There are five spots we hooked fish behind the airport to the take-out. At the bottom of each riffle starts a hole that is quite obvious and holds fish in optimal water temperatures. The last hole is notorious, and called Slaughterhouse. The take-out ramp (on the map it's called "Ahsahka Access") is about half a mile of frog water downriver. Adding this stretch to the Zans drift is handy when there is a lot of fishing pressure. More than once I have put-in and shot right down several miles to Fords Creek or lower to start fishing. This put me almost half a day ahead of most and took me that extra 2.0 miles on down past where most are taking out.

Upper river steelhead "hole".

The sixth drift is Zans to Slaughterhouse = 7.35 miles (1.37 boat hours per fish) and is a combination of the fourth and fifth drifts.

Chapter 16

Lower River Favorite Drifts

"Don't leave fish to find fish."
—Mike Smith

I had to consciously remind myself of this. We would be in an average spot and hook a fish or two and I would start thinking of all the "better" places down the river below us that were hydraulically similar. If this spot was good, those spots would be REALLY good! You know how this ends...after we had moved and had no action, somebody in the boat would say: "We never should have left the place we were hooking those fish." Moving on can be a tough call to make in a drift boat because you can't go back up a rapid. You can always eliminate a place you were going to fish down river. But in general, "Don't leave fish to find fish."

"October Sunrise"

Photo by Mike McElhatton www.digitalartsphotography.com

The following are the boat hours per fish we hooked, by drift in the lower river.

Lower River Drift	Boat Hours per hook up
Pink House to Peck (Harpers Bend)	1.64
Peck to Lenore	1.75
Peck to Lava Rock	1.50
Lenore to Cherrylane	1.73
Hog Island to Steelhead Park	1.51

As I suggested in the previous chapter, do not take this as commentary that fishing is better in one drift over another. The longer the drift and travel time between spots, the higher the hours per fish. Generally, it is farther between spots in the lower river than the upper and thus the very slight differences in hours per fish. But most importantly, we did about the same in the upper and lower river because most of the time we were fishing similar conditions.

The lower river is more of a "flat-bottomed bowl shape". The holes are much less distinct, longer, wider and generally deeper. Fish in the lower river are generally spread out more than in the upper river. But the lower river also has rapids, holes and channels and submerged structure that concentrate and hold fish. These places are not as visible in the lower river. There are six drifts we fished.

The first is Pink House to Peck (Harpers Bend) = 5.1 miles (1.64 boat hours per fish). This is the most heavily fished stretch of water above Lewiston, and as a result the one I fished the least. We have hooked fish in 15 different locations in this drift. It is immediately down river from the hatchery with nice paved ramps, camping and restroom facilities. You are now in motors water and I have seen several drift boats bite off two sections of this stretch using a motor to quickly get through the frog water and fish down 10 miles to Lenore. The famous holes like McGill are obvious due to the boats and bank fishermen there. It is bigger water than above as the

Tailouts and runs concentrate fish.

Dworshak Dam flow has been added here. Tailouts at the bottom and runs at the top of each hole seem to concentrate fish in these big holes but, when the fishing is good, we watched people landing fish all over the place.

When fishing in a crowd I liked to be above or well below them and closer to shore than normal in a channel. Also helps keep from getting run over! Any shade on the highway side of the river in a slot produced well—particularly on bright sunny days. I also liked fishing with smaller lures in these situations. When you get to a long, slow, glassy hole, row around and find a slot 4'-10' deep and fish down through it and, as always, don't ignore points in good water.

The second drift, Peck (Harpers Bend) to Lenore = 5.7 miles (1.75 boat hours per fish). I liked this drift because you could fish in holes from put-in to take-out and the spots are not far apart. There are two Lenore ramps so make sure you shuttle across the bridge to the upper ramp. We hooked fish in 16 different locations on this drift.

Much the same as the previous description but the good spots are more obvious in this drift if you fish the tailouts, slots, submerged boulder fields, runs, point's (particularly) and shade. Stay in 4'-10' of water as there is a lot more that is deeper. When you get to the last two holes, don't miss the two sharp points sticking out from the highway side with good six to eight feet deep water and current above Lenore. When you see them, you will probably make a bee-line right to them.

Fishing the points in good water is productive.

STRIKING STEELHEAD

The third drift from the Lenore Rest Area to "Lava Rock" = about 1.0 mile, another quickie. We have caught fish in five places in this little stretch. The area above the tailout at Agatha is good, as are the points above it. Once through the rapid there are Lava Rock points on the right that hold fish and the unmarked, crude "sand" ramp (above) is on the left (4WD).

Be careful pulling out of this place with your boat and trailer as it is straight off the sand onto Hwy. 12 on a blind curve.

The fourth drift, Peck (Harpers Bend) to Lava Rock = 7.5 miles (1.50 boat hours per fish) and is a combination of the second and third drifts above—plus about .8 miles between the upper and lower ramps.

Mike Smith.

The fifth drift, Lenore Rest Area to Cherrylane = 6.8 miles (1.73 boat hours per fish). The river seems to flatten out and get wider in this long drift. We hooked fish in 13 different places in this drift. If the wind is going to blow from the west, go somewhere else or eat your Wheaties before you launch. It's a pretty good pull between holes in the lower part of this drift. Not a lot of shade either. Now that I've talked you out of it, Agatha is a good spot, as are the lava-rock points on the right in the next hole downriver. Then fish tailouts and runs in the next couple holes. These are long holes and the fish are usually where the water temperature places them. When you get to Cold Springs, fish it high and don't miss the slot above the Cherrylane Bridge.

The sixth drift, Upper Hog Island to Steelhead Park = 5.3 Miles (1.51 boat hours per fish). This is the drift I used in special situations, primarily during late August to early September with the Dworshak high-flow scenario. I would have fished it more but it's about 30 miles down (one way) from where I stayed in Orofino. But there is no doubt it's a good place all season. This is not heavily-used drift-boat water and as a result shuttles require imagination (The Red Lion-Lewiston shuttled me one day in their airport bus.) There are not many places that have a boat dock at the take-out! The holes are huge and the river is deeper overall down there (perfect for drift fishing from a power boat). As a result, I fished the edges—particularly points, runs and tailouts in three to ten feet of water—and ignored the deeper water for the reasons mentioned earlier. We hooked steelhead in 10 spots on this drift.

This drift is an example of special situations: in 12,300 CFS flow one 92-degree, late-August day we hooked 11 fish in this drift—including a double at Hatwai Creek. We hooked fish almost everywhere we fished. That same day I pulled over and watched three fly-fishermen hook steelhead in the Coyote Fishnet area. A few of our fish were "B"s. There is definitely a Slimerocket party going on there when they are dumping Dworshak.

Chapter 17

Plan

*E*very morning while the coffee was percolating, I would check the weather forecast, then "Real Time" water temperature and flow readings at http://waterdata.usgs.gov/nwis for Orofino (upper river), site #13340000, and at Peck (lower river), site #13341050 (you can also pick around on the site and find this information without these numbers). I also looked at the flow graph to determine whether the flow line was "Rising, Falling or Level". As mentioned before, the fishing was better if the river was level or falling. You will also see the temperature difference between Orofino and Peck due to the Dworshak Dam discharge.

Another little trick was to check the flows of the Lochsa, Selway and South Fork Clearwater and add them up to give me an idea of what was headed my way. These three are not all the flow coming into the fishing water in the upper river but they comprised the overwhelming majority. You have to assume the person operating the valve at Dworshak Dam will behave themselves and discharge will remain relatively steady, which it usually does from October on. But in September, if this is going to be a day breaker, you better call and ask.

After accumulating this data for several years, I began to use this real-time data to decide whether to fish up river or down river. Then, as I mentioned before, flip a coin and pick your drift. We wouldn't kill ourselves to get out on the water at the crack of dawn—particularly when the anchor rope was frozen to the floor of the boat.

If you want steelhead counts over Lower Granite Dam, go to The Fish Passage Center web site for daily updates at http://www.fpc.org/currentdaily/HistFishTwo7day-ytdAdults.htm

It's good to know what flow is headed your way. The upper Lochsa River.

Chapter 18

A Perfect Steelhead World: Top 60 Days

After 10 years' involvement in fish politics and 30 years on rivers, it's hard not to imagine what it "used to be like" before dams and the hatcheries necessary to replace the loss of wild production. When there were so many chinook, coho and sockeye salmon that steelhead really were a nuisance during the fall salmon fishery. Back when Idaho rivers were full of spring, summer and fall chinook salmon, from summer through fall in the most beautiful scenery and water on the planet. Back when only a few hardy souls that appreciated the "sport" of a big, jumping, wild steelhead fished for them in relative obscurity and solitude in October and November, while everyone else was up in the woods hunting.

Back to earth… Our perfect steelhead world would be the best days we had during this period. I decided to see what the average conditions were during our 60 best days on the river during this 18-year period. I defined "best" as the number of fish hooked.

Where water temperatures were recorded as a range, I averaged to one number. Where a few flow numbers (in the early years) were recorded generically, I assigned a number that would correspond with what we know now. Finally, we had to have fished at least four hours to qualify as a day. Therefore these top 60 days include a few special situations. Here is the table of data with the averages at the bottom:

Top 60 Days	1988	to	2005		
Date	Hours Fished	Fish - On	Hrs./Fish	Water Temp	Flow CFS
14-Oct-04	6	18	0.33	49	2360
31-Oct-05	7	16	0.44	43	1400
26-Oct-00	8	14	0.57	43	4000
06-Nov-01	8	14	0.57	41	3250
28-Sep-00	8	13	0.62	50	3000
25-Sep-02	7	13	0.54	52	2900
17-Oct-96	8	12	0.67	46	3350
19-Oct-00	8	12	0.67	48	3600
15-Sep-01	8	12	0.67	53	2650
28-Sep-02	8	12	0.67	49	2970
02-Oct-02	8	12	0.67	50	3270
21-Sep-00	7	11	0.64	52	3200
27-Oct-00	7	11	0.64	42	3900
25-Aug-01	7	11	0.64	52	12300
05-Nov-01	8	11	0.73	42	3500

12-Dec-98	8	**10**	0.80	38	4800
20-Oct-00	7	**10**	0.70	48	3880
03-Oct-01	7	**10**	0.70	49	2470
19-Oct-01	8	**10**	0.80	45	3200
09-Oct-02	8	**10**	0.80	49	3140
12-Oct-89	5	**9**	0.56	**55**	1900
23-Oct-89	7	**9**	0.78	46	1900
19-Oct-91	5	**9**	0.56	51	2900
08-Oct-92	8	**9**	0.89	50	2900
04-Oct-01	7	**9**	0.78	48	2800
07-Nov-01	5	**9**	0.56	42	3000
21-Sep-02	7	**9**	0.78	50	3050
22-Sep-02	6	**9**	0.67	51	2980
24-Sep-02	7	**9**	0.78	51	2900
17-Oct-92	7	**8**	0.88	48	2900
13-Dec-98	4	**8**	0.50	37	5000
07-Oct-00	8	**8**	1.00	46	2800
29-Oct-02	6	**8**	0.75	40	1150
14-Nov-02	7	**8**	0.88	39	1970
10-Nov-04	6	**8**	0.75	45	2300
14-Oct-89	6	**7**	0.86	**53**	1900
05-Nov-92	6	**7**	0.86	43	4400
06-Nov-92	7	**7**	1.00	42	4600
12-Nov-92	8	**7**	1.14	40	4600
04-Nov-93	8	**7**	1.14	44	1900
16-Dec-98	5	**7**	0.71	38	4000
25-Oct-99	8	**7**	1.14	47	2750
29-Sep-00	7	**7**	1.00	48	3000
12-Oct-00	5	**7**	0.71	48	2180
02-Nov-00	7	**7**	1.00	41	3400
05-Oct-01	7	**7**	1.00	48	2450
03-Oct-03	8	**7**	1.14	52	2800
09-Nov-04	6	**7**	0.86	45	3000
03-Nov-88	7	**6**	1.17	45	3000
13-Oct-89	7	**6**	1.17	**53**	1800
26-Oct-89	7	**6**	1.17	45	2000
13-Nov-89	5	**6**	0.83	47	5400
06-Dec-90	4	**6**	0.67	40	2100
07-Dec-90	5	**6**	0.83	40	2100
10-Oct-91	6	**6**	1.00	55	2960
09-Oct-92	9	**6**	1.50	53	2900
06-Nov-93	8	**6**	1.33	41	1900
03-Nov-95	4	**6**	0.67	36	3000
27-Oct-98	7	**6**	1.17	47	2400
31-Oct-98	6	**6**	1.00	44	2750
13-Oct-00	7	**6**	1.17	48	2700

AVERAGE	416	540	0.77	47	2967
	Hours	Fish	Hrs./fish	Wtr.Temp	Flow

31 of these 60 days were in October.
15 of these 60 days were in November.
9 of these 60 days were in September.
5 of these 60 days were in December.

1. On these 60 best days we averaged hooking a fish every 45 minutes.
2. The average water temperature was 47 degrees F.
3. The average flow was 2,967 CFS (I did not separate upper or lower river flows).
4. 32 days were on the upper river, 28 days were on the lower river.
5. Of all the fish hooked in my fish log, 46.4% were hooked in these 60 days.
6. We averaged nine fish a day on these 60 days. (It takes a while to land these things and to float six miles!)
7. 34 of the Best 60 Days were in the last 6 years I kept records, between 2000-2005. Meaning only 26 were in the first 12 years between 1988-1999. (We were getting much more efficient, opportunistic, wasting less time. We were fishing higher probability times, hydraulics, temperature and flow conditions. The falling hours-per-fish trend line in the Chapter 4 charts bear this out as, well, a long, expensive, time-consuming learning curve)
8. The "fish" numbers are understated a bit as I only recorded fish landed in 1988 to early 1991. (Yes, knowing the "landed rate," I could extrapolate more "probable" fish we hooked. But that seems more like something a congressman would do than a guy writing an honest fishing book.)
9. **It's not in the table, but the air temperature rose to be warmer than the water on 58 of these 60 days.**

All these Best Days were spread out in the drifts discussed in Chapters 15 and 16. There were also a couple double-digit fish days in September from Upper Hog Island to Steelhead Park drift.

Update: October 21, 2011

In Chapter 5 I mentioned that due to the higher, cooler flow and therefore faster migration travel times, the 2011 catch-and-release season should be a barn burner. I could not travel to the Clearwater until October 16. The first two days, October 17-18, we fished a rising flow of 3200-3300 CFS of stained (the color of weak tea) water resulting in a total of eight hookups in 14 hours of fishing. October 19, fishing a falling, clearing river at 2800-2500 CFS resulted in a day that would replace one of "The Top 60 Days"—and one of "The 6 Best Days" at the end of the book. We hooked 16 steelhead in seven hours of fishing. We fished the same drift all three days. Comparing the conditions of Wednesday, October 19 to the table averages above, they are almost identical.

16 Fish Hooked

Date: October 19, 2011
Section: Upper River; Zans to Slaughterhouse
Weather: Clear-Partly Cloudy
Air Temperature: 42-65 F°
Wind: Still
Flow CFS: 2800-2500
Rising, Falling, Steady: Falling (had been falling from 3300)
Clarity: 7-8 feet (back to normal)
Water Temp. Start: 49 F°
Water Temp. End: 50 F°
Colors: Blue and Green
Fished With: John Kelly and Bill Eggleston
Lures: Blue Hawg Boss hooked 6, Green Rattle Tot hooked 5, Blue 35 Hot Shot (no Shrimp) hooked 1, Green 35 Hot Shot (no shrimp) hooked 4.

Comments: Starting about 10:00 a.m. we hooked fish everywhere we fished, including the Golf Club for the first time in years. Had a double and landed both. Had two rods go down at once two other times but only hooked one of the two. Fish were bigger than previous two days and one jumped 11 (that's eleven) times. Last 6 fish came from a back-eddy seam. We would fish half-way down the fast-water run then pull the boat into the back-eddy. As the lures swung downstream and came through the seam, both rods would hook-up. We did this 3 times in a row. This could be a new technique for us, or just pure luck. Could not fish last two spots as someone else was already there... it was almost dark anyway. All fish were released...about 50/50 hatchery/wild. No scent used. This was an incredible day.

In my fish log, in addition to the general data, each of these fish would have had an entry for the lure, color, time of day, the hole, shrimp (or not) and scent used (or not)...a total of 96 entries.

We hooked 16 of these and released all 12 we landed Oct. 19, 2011.

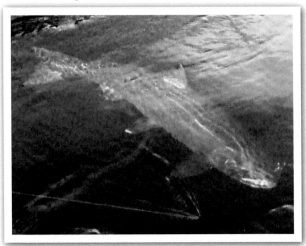

Chapter 19

Our Technique & Some Rambling Opinions

Don't Waste Your Time

Once we shoved off, the water temperature and flow pretty much formulated where I spent time in a hole. We were looking for places in a hole or characteristics of temperature, flow and structure that would concentrate fish. For instance in 50-degree water, I would plan on spending more time in faster water, fast-water seams, higher in holes or the lower, faster parts of tailouts, and less time in the slow-water middle. Cold water would be the exact opposite. All of this is simply trying to increase probability. Here is the cover picture again.

That fish came right out of the slick, just off the tip of the oar sticking out (bottom right) in the picture, at the top of the hole in four feet of 50-degree water maybe 15 feet from the bank.

Left to right: John Kelly, Randy Dawson, wild Slimerocket.

In warm water, it is more probable that a steelhead will be in the run at the top of a hole, in seams next to fast water or lying under the rapid in fast water. In cold water, it is more probable a steelhead will be in slower current farther down, on the edges of positive flow or right on bottom. That doesn't mean they are ALL there. I fish most of a hole regardless but I do not spend a lot of time and waste a lot of energy where I do not "think" they will be. We did not shake off any loners that were where "they were not supposed to be." And yes, like you, I have caught steelhead where they should not have been, but that is the exception not the high probability. (I know, that exception weighed 18 pounds.) As the temperatures and flows change, the steelheads' holding areas change. Like any other kind of fishing, once you hook a fish or two, keep that hydraulic "pattern" going until it quits working. Often, it does not quit working.

Except in fast water, we would anchor the boat well above the spot we thought would hold fish. This allows everybody to get set up, ready and lures put out about the same distance. Often we would anchor above a spot in two feet of quick water to let the lures down into (what we knew to be) four to eight feet of water. Once I pulled anchor and began to ease us down, we would often hook-up quickly. Point being, we did not row in on top of them and drop 25 pounds of lead to the bottom of the river on a rope.

Territorial Squabbles

The two people in this picture would sit in my boat and squabble all day about anything. But I believe Clearwater steelhead strike out of a territorial instinct. They are on their spawning run. They are not eating. They are like a yard dog, lying somewhere comfortable until something irritating violates their space, then they attack. If the intruder leaves quickly, they just lay there. I think in warm water their patience level with an intruder is shorter and their attack trigger is tripped quicker. And usually in warm water it is an attack. In warmer water we fished faster water and fished a little faster through a hole, and subsequently covered more water

In cold water they seem to be not nearly as territorial and had much more patience. When they would finally decide to clear the area, they seemed to merely mouth

Chris Oakes and Pamela Magers with Mr. Hatchery Slimerocket.

the lure/shrimp combo and "move it" away. The strikes we do get in water temperatures in the low 40s or less are generally "tap-tap-tap" and slow take-downs, or the rod tip just stops its slow vibration, moves down a few inches and stays there. As a result, we fished the slower water in the hole and fished it much more slowly. In a lot of these cold-water, slow-flow spots I could hardly even row without going upstream and it might take a minute or more for the lures to float 50-60 feet downstream. We would anchor and sit there with the lures out, maybe five to ten minutes, then let out another few feet of anchor rope moving the boat and lures down a little or pull the anchor, move over a bit and anchor again. We hooked a lot of steelhead doing this in cold water.

Water Depth

Steelhead feel safest at the bottom of the river. We did best in water depths of three to ten feet, as that is the depth at which the lures seemed to be most effective. Deeper water was usually too slow to work a lure. In a few places where much deeper water was fast enough for us to fish, I don't think the lures got down to a depth that triggered any territorial instinct from steelhead lying on the bottom of the river. Some annoying, rattling thing coming down the river 10 feet deep over the top of a steelhead lying 20 feet deep is not going to elicit much reaction. This is another reason people are successful drift fishing—they are fishing on the bottom. We did not waste much time in 12'-30'-deep holes watching our rod tips as not much ever happened. Again, probability (or get out your drift gear).

Billy Myers and his first steelhead.

Back 'Em Down

Twenty-plus years ago I attended a presentation by Buzz Ramsey of Luhr Jensen. Buzz discussed more effective back-trolling when the lures were out about the same distance. I just started doing this without a whole lot of thought. But if the territorial theory is correct, it makes perfect sense. If they move over to avoid one lure, another is in their face. We have had a smack on one rod then immediately had the other rod bury over the front of the boat. We would get a lot of these smacks before a hook-up that may have been a fish slapping the lure with their tail. Would it have happened if the lures were out different distances? Who knows? But it happened much too often to dismiss as coincidence. I think having two lures out about the same distance raises the probability of a hook-up. I think it is also fairly obvious that steelhead will back down from lures, particularly if two are bearing down at them and they will not just sidestep one. If they keep backing down, the tailout is a back-stop. They will not go back down the rapid and often attack.

Air Temperature

One of my friends was strident about air versus water temperature. The theory is that steelhead turn on once the air gets warmer than the water. I only kept daily beginning and ending ambient air temperatures (not by fish). In Chapter 16: The 60 Best Days, on 58 of the 60 days the air temperature rose above the water temperature. I mentioned earlier about how a sunny day can warm the cold water up a degree or two and really turn the fish on. Maybe

Steve Jordan.

Chris Oakes (left) and Jeff Pryor (right).

the direction that the water temperature is moving is what this is all about. In Chapter 20, the six best days were when the air temperature warmed past the water temperature rather early in the day, and in two of the three "El Skunkos" I included in the last chapter the air never got warmer than the water. Another reason not to get out too early in November!

On the USGS website you can see real-time ongoing graphs of water temperatures. I probably could have saved time, lowered my hours per fish and had an extra cup of coffee in the morning if I had paid more attention to this in November. You probably never thought of sleeping until 7:00, going to breakfast and getting on the river mid-morning after everybody else is three hours gone down the river... then, hooking a bunch of steelhead they floated over. When John, Mike and I would compare notes at the end of a day we all fished, it was amazing how often we all started hooking fish about the same hour of the day—on different drifts—miles apart.

Steelhead Sweat?

Another friend swears that steelhead "sweat" during the fight and that this "sweat" or slime puts a danger smell in the water that warns all his buddies. This may well be true. We have noticed that after hooking a fish in a hole and fighting it around for a while further action in that same spot takes some time. Perhaps with this "sweat theory" in the back of my mind, when we would hook-up I would always row the boat over to a back-eddy or bank in calm water and try to get the fish out of the main thread of the hole. This calm water also made it easier to deal with unhooking and releasing the fish. After release, we would take our time, take pictures, check the line for frays, re-tie the clip, toast the fish gods, give the oarsman a break, whatever. Then slip back out and start fishing again and sometimes hook another. But it seemed like when we would hook a big wild fish that ran all over the hole, jumped half a

114

dozen times and just tore things up, that was generally the end of activity for that hole. I would hit the hole another lick or two and move on. Probabilities again. What is the probability of hooking another fish in that hole after all the commotion? Could also be why taking 15 minutes to row back up and come back down through the hole a second time was sometimes successful.

> *"New opinions are always suspected and usually opposed because they are not already common."*
> —John Lock

Gotta Be First?

Fishing writer, fly tier and excellent fly-fisherman Marv Taylor fished with me a couple times on the Clearwater. He had a real thing about being first in the hole. Marv told me that when fishing with Ted Trueblood, Ted always said he would take the first 10 casts and Marv could have the next 90. Another friend has always contended there are only so many "biters" in a hole and that being the first there is best. There must be a shred of truth in this as I never fished a day with a guide on the Olympic Peninsula in Washington that I was not up looking for breakfast at 3:30 a.m. so nobody would launch before us! If there is a steady parade of boats in a drift and holes are getting hit every 20 minutes this is probably true. But as John Kelly has said to me many times, "Hey, fish swim around." New fish come into a hole and ultimately find that same comfort zone that was vacated.

Look close, we were not first in this spot.

Given enough time in a day, I don't think the guy that went down an hour or two ahead of me is affecting my results. And odds are high he is fishing a different way in different little spots with different gear than I am anyway. Being there first certainly doesn't hurt. Knowing the conditions and fishing them is much more important.

The "Good Spots" Change (Again, but with a story)

From year to year, the spring thaw and accompanying high water can change a hole. This effect is nowhere near as pronounced on the Clearwater as on coastal streams where holes can vanish and new ones appear from storm to storm. But we have had many of our places produce one year and do nothing the next. Due to the type of rock that is prevalent in the area, the Clearwater River seldom changes visibly but even a slight hydraulic change will move the fish around. The tailout by the Orofino Golf Course is a classic example. We did not ever fish it—too shallow and too slow. One day while I was waiting to meet somebody, I put a lure out just killing time—and hooked two fish there the next hour. Mike and John were really surprised. For years we floated over this spot on the way down river. The rest of that year "The Golf Club" was automatic—there's even a picture of a double we hooked there in the final chapter of this book. I don't know that any of us have hooked a fish there since that year. On the surface it looks the same today as it did back then. This is why anglers need to go down the river, look around, be mindful of water depth and fish all the likely looking water while there is time to fish. This is the only way to know the hot spots from season to season.

Pick Pockets

My favorite spots are "pocket water"—anywhere. And there is no better way to fish pocket water than in a drift boat. Pocket water is too small for bigger boats, too big a hassle to access from the bank to fish one tiny little spot, difficult to cast to and snaggy. But you can back-troll a lure through it from a drift boat with none of these issues.

This trip into that pocket was good for two (Perry Gossett's fish).

Pockets are easy to spot and it does not take but a few minutes to find out if anybody is home. Think about it. There is a long, shallow, rocky riffle with a little green slot six feet wide, three feet deep and just a few yards or more long with some chop—or a slick. Where is a fish going to take a blow going up through that riffle? Once he is in there catching his breath, where can he go when you run a Hawg Boss in there?

John Kelly and I were floating from Pink House to Peck one day. There was a lot of river traffic and several power boats already running back and forth drift fishing a great slot of deeper, faster water at the top of the long glassy hole above Peck. It would have been rude to crowd ourselves into the middle of all that and try to fish it the way we wanted to. We noticed a couple of small "slicks" just above the point that we had never fished way over on the left. I picked my way down through the

James Gross.

shallow side of the riffle and got above the slicks and finagled around so John could get his lure out and down to the slicks. Three straight times we hooked up in there, and I did it again the next time I floated that stretch. There is no way anyone could have fished that pocket in anything other than a drift boat, back-trolling. Another place to find pockets is just off to the side and on the seam of really fast water.

An example is the rapid above Slaughterhouse that has a little pocket maybe 30 feet long on the right side about half way down that was good for a fish almost every time we went through it. It is squirrely rowing once you get stopped as your left arm is going full tilt pulling the oars on the edge of the rollers while your right arm is pushing the oars fast in the back-eddy to keep the boat straight. In these spots the fisherman in the front can help by holding the rod and moving the rod tip to keep the line and lure in the seam. But when a big Slimerocket tries to separate the rod and reel from the fisherman's grasp, runs out in the rapid and takes off downriver, I love to hear those words: "I'm running out of line!"

There is no better way to capitalize on a steelhead's territorial instincts than pocket water. Around boulders there are always pockets and the short seams downstream from them. The small dips in the river bottom in front of and just behind points—right up next to the bank. When there is a lot of pressure on the river I think these little pockets are even better and seldom get fished. They are easily spotted, easily fished and are surprising; these small pockets really increase probability and hook-ups.

Chapter 20

Funny, Amazing and Just Plain Stupid

*A*nyone who has spent any time on a river fishing steelhead knows that sometimes "stuff" just happens…to some more than others.

Fishing by myself one day I had broken a rod trying to move the boat with my rod in a holder and a fish on. I re-rigged with the spare rod I had brought. I moved down to a back-eddy and put a lure in the water out the right side of the boat in the seam next to the really fast water of the rapid going out of the Slaughterhouse hole. In 15 years I had floated over the top of this small little run (pocket water) and never fished it. The rod almost jerked out of my hand and when I set the hook…the rod sounded like a firecracker when it broke. The fish jumped and was gone. There I sat in a drift boat with nobody in sight, still anchored, in a spot full of steelhead and no rod. I had hooked fish almost everywhere I fished that day and figured this was a perfect way to end a day. Two days later, Chuck and Tommy from Oregon went on the same drift with me. When we stopped there, I told them what had happened to me. Chuck proceeded to have the exact same experience. I don't think Chuck thought it was funny when his rod snapped but I had to row over and anchor I was laughing so hard. The TBR hole!

Bill Eggleston exercises another one.

Fishing with Bill Eggleston one day in September (catch and release) we had hooked three fish, but had not gotten one to the boat to photograph. After losing the third one, Bill said "Geez, I can't believe we are that bad today." We regrouped, pulled back out in the current and Bill put the lures out. There was a boulder sticking out of the water in the middle of a good run just below us. I eased the lures down and got Bill's lure right by the rock. Bill's rod slammed down, he set the hook and the fish came barreling out of the water, landed on top of the rock, flexed, and the lure came flying back through the air at us. The look on Bill's face had me back over to the side, anchored again, doubled over with laughter.

Pam and I were fishing a hole called Richardson's (the third hole upriver from Orofino) one afternoon when she hooked a nice fish that immediately took to the air.

A big bald eagle appeared out of nowhere and swooped down at the splash, soared back up and came down and did it again when the fish jumped a second time. I rowed us over to one side

in calmer water, the fish stayed down but the eagle kept circling around close overhead. When Pam got the fish about 20 feet from the boat, it came up where we could see it again and down came the eagle again—swooping down trying to grab Pam's fish.

Being 20 feet from a big bald eagle that wants what you have is too close. We could hear the sound of the air going across the eagle's wings when it swooped down. This bird was not concerned with us in the least. I could see big-trouble potential all over this deal. I had Pam horse the fish around to the other side of the boat in the 20 feet of distance between the boat and bank so I could release it with a little protection (and not get my ass kicked by a bird). The fish was still quite lively and shot out of my hands, went under the boat and back down into the river as the eagle hovered overhead. It helps to know when to let someone else have the hole. We went on down the river to the next spot.

The Hoh Story

This is not a Clearwater story, but it is amusing. We lived in Boise, Idaho for a period of time and mid-summer temperatures were in the 100's. My wife, Pam, and I wanted to find a cool place to go fishing one hot 4th of July weekend. We decided to go to the Hoh River on the Olympic Peninsula in Forks, Washington.

I called a drift-boat guide I knew there—Steve Bogart—and asked him to take us fishing for a couple of days. Steve explained it was too late for salmon and too early for steelhead but if we were hell-bent on going he would take us down the river. We were hell-bent on some cool weather so off we went.

It was warm in Forks, Washington too. Not often a person fishes the Hoh River in shorts and a T-shirt. The first three places we fished, we caught chinook salmon. The next three places we fished, we hooked steelhead. Steve could not believe it and we were not expecting much either. It was quite a day.

When we arrived at the take-out, Steve pulled the boat up on the rocks. He and I took the salmon out of the fish box and began to clean them on the edge of the river bank. We were bent over doing our chore and out of the corner of my eye I saw something move. Steve and I both stood up as a woman walked down to the river bank, completely naked, waded into the river right beside us and began bathing.

Steve and I stood there speechless when Pam piped up, "You guys better be careful or you'll lose a finger cleaning those fish." We quickly went back to our work. After we had loaded the boat and were driving off, Pam turned around and said to me: "You will never go steelhead fishing without me again."

On a bright, early October day, we were fishing between Lenore and Cherrylane in a spot that had good flow and chop. We had fished it before but had never done real well there. Pam jerked back on her rod and said. "There he is." Seconds later, Rick jerked back on his rod and yelled, "We've got a double." Man, was I excited! A double is rare. I rowed over to calmer water and anchored and watched these two fight their fish. Then they begin talking about how the fish were not fighting like steelhead usually do. I stood up and saw both their lines going down into the water pointing in the same direction and told them they had each other. Both swore they had a fish. Less than a minute later they pulled up a beautiful 37-inch wild male steelhead with both of their lures in his mouth, one in each side. Don't tell me wild fish are not more aggressive. I didn't get a picture as I needed to get this guy back into the gene pool as fast as possible!

This One Ranks as Just Plain Stupid

Pam Magers and Bill Eggleston were in the front of the boat one hot, early October day as we floated from Peck to Lenore. They had plenty of action and as a result I hadn't had my set-up in the water much at all. It was in the 80's with not a cloud in the sky and I was getting pretty warm rowing in fast water, even in a pair of shorts and a T-shirt. We shot down to the second hole above the Lenore ramp we called "Carbody" (don't ask). It is always shady and a couple points stick out into the river from the highway side. Like most other places, some years it is really good and others it's just so-so. But it was a shady, much cooler place to fish.

I fished them down into the hole about half way and anchored so I could put my rod out too. I put my lure out short about 40 feet, put the rod in the rod holder and sat there about a minute before my rod got a violent hit. I reached over with one hand, jerked the rod out of the holder and back to set the hook in one motion. As I pulled back, the fish went the other way. My hands were wet from the anchor rope and the combination of the force and slick, wet cork on the rod handle wrenched the rod and reel right out of my hand into the river. (Bear with me here, it gets stupid-er.)

I saw the rod and reel on the surface scooting toward the front of the boat as the fish towed it downriver and then went airborne. I dove toward the front of the boat, over Bill and over the side just enough to get a couple fingers on it as it slipped away, down river and out of sight. Then I realized I had my right arm over the front of the boat, my right leg hooked over the top of the gunwale and the rest of me in the river. With the help of adrenaline, Bill and Pam, somehow I got back into the boat without turning it over and putting everybody and everything in the river. My hair was even wet. (Through all this Bill pointed out that the big steelhead was still jumping way downriver with my lure in his mouth.) I couldn't figure out why my chest hurt until I saw the top part of my depth finder dangling from wires and realized I had broken it off with my chest when I "landed".

I pulled the anchor and got a 20-minute floating lecture—in stereo—until we got to the take-out at Lenore. My defense was weak: I told them I could replace the rod and reel, but they don't make those green Rattle Tots anymore.

Chapter 21

The Six Best and The Ugly

The Six Best Days

18 Fish Hooked

Date:	October 14, 2004
Section:	Upper River; Zans to Slaughterhouse
Weather:	Clear
Air Temperature:	42-70 F°
Wind:	Light breeze
Flow CFS:	2360
Rising, Falling, Steady:	Steady (been falling from 3200)
Clarity:	7-8 feet
Water Temp Start:	47 F°
Water Temp End:	50 F°
Colors:	Pink or anything else we used
Fished With:	Pam Magers and Mickey Turnbow

Comments: Only reason to leave anywhere was to get down the river before dark. We didn't even fish the last two holes due to darkness. Most spots we didn't even have to pull up anchor after getting set to hook-up.

16 Fish Hooked

Date:	October 31, 2005
Section:	Upper River; Zans to Airport
Weather:	Light rain all day
Air Temperature:	40-46 F°
Wind:	None
Flow CFS:	1400 (banged some rocks)
Rising, Falling, Steady:	Falling (been falling from 3400 week before)
Clarity:	6 feet
Water Temp Start:	43 F°
Water Temp End:	43 F°
Colors:	Mae West & Purple
Fished With:	Pam Magers and Mike Smith

Comments: PAM'S 50th Birthday. Mike gave her a Mae West Hawg marked "FAB 50"...she hooked 8 of 16 on it. Too late to fish Bill's or Carcass holes. Fish everywhere. Banged lots of rocks at this flow.

14 Fish Hooked

Date:	October 26, 2000
Section:	Upper River; Golf Course to Slaughterhouse, shot 2 miles down to Golf Course from Zans before start.
Weather:	Cloudy
Air Temperature:	40-55 F°
Wind:	None
Flow CFS:	3900
Rising, Falling, Steady:	Falling (been falling from 4400 week before)
Clarity:	6 feet
Water Temp Start:	43 F°
Water Temp End:	43 F°
Colors:	Red 8, Purple 6
Fished With:	Bill Eggleston and Bill Guerhke (pictured)

*A double, a rare event...
and an even rarer picture of one.*

Comments: First two fish were a double at the Golf Club tailout. Fish were everywhere. We almost had another double at the trap club. Fish bit all day.

14 Fish Hooked

Date:	November 6, 2001
Section:	Upper River; Zans to Slaughterhouse
Weather:	Clear
Air Temperature:	48 F° (p.m.)
Wind:	Still till 2:00, then blew 15-20
Flow CFS:	3250
Rising, Falling, Steady:	Steady
Clarity:	7 feet
Water Temp Start:	41 F°
Water Temp End:	42 F°
Colors:	Black, Purple & Red/Black
Fished With:	Pam Magers and Bill Eggleston

Comments: Fish were caught all day long. All males, 34-36" long...?? Amazing fishing; fish everywhere. 14th fish caught at Bill's...Hawgs & MagWart, Purple, Black, or Red/Black, shrimp and pops.

This one deserves the story. The day before we had hooked 11 and released all we landed. That evening, the three of us decided we needed some smoked steelhead for the holidays. So we set out the next day to get 6 keepers to have smoked.

Six keepers that got smoked and one of the culprits: Bill Eggleston. We had to cull through 14 to get six because eight were wild.

13 Fish Hooked

Date:	September 28, 2000
Section:	Lower River; Lenore to Cherrylane
Weather:	Clear to Partly Cloudy
Air Temperature:	46-72 F°
Wind:	None
Flow CFS:	3000
Rising, Falling, Steady:	Steady
Clarity:	7-8 feet
Water Temp Start:	50 F°
Water Temp End:	50 F°
Colors:	Pink 8, Chartreuse Clown 5
Fished With:	Pam Magers and Bill Eggleston

Comments: Nobody in this section but us. Could have spent all day in first four holes and taken out at Satellite Flats. No time to fish last two holes.

13 Fish Hooked

Date:	September 25, 2002
Section:	Lower River; Peck to Lenore
Weather:	Clear
Air Temperature:	45-75 F°
Wind:	10-15 upriver in p.m.
Flow CFS:	2900
Rising, Falling, Steady:	Steady
Clarity:	Clear
Water Temp Start:	50 F°
Water Temp End:	50 F°
Colors:	Magnum Wiggle Warts Silver/Red, Silver/Orange
Fished With:	Stu Kestner

Comments: Hard to fish in afternoon with upriver wind and low flow. Last four fish came off two left points at Lenore that I had never fished before.

Three Ugly Days: We Knew Better, but Went Anyway

El Skunko (What the hell were we thinking?)

Date: November 25, 1992
Section: Upper River; 5 Mile to Zans
Weather: Clear
Air Temperature: 15 F°
Wind: None
Flow CFS: "Very Low"
Rising, Falling, Steady: Steady
Clarity: 7-8 feet
Water Temp Start: 33 F°
Water Temp End: 35 F°
Colors:
Fished With: Pam Magers & John Kelly
Comments: No comments, the picture (below) says enough.

When you fish in this, you are officially hard-core.

El Skunko (It was so nasty, I didn't even take a picture)_____

Date:	November 27, 1992
Section:	Lower River; Lenore to Cherrylane
Weather:	Snow...lots of it
Air Temperature:	32 F°
Wind:	15-25 mph
Flow CFS:	"Very, very low"
Rising, Falling, Steady:	Falling (from 3400 week before)
Clarity:	"Very Clear; Upper River Frozen
Water Temp Start:	38 F°
Water Temp End:	38 F°
Colors:	
Fished With:	Pam Magers and Bruce Cushman

Comments: Snowed all day. Had to "shovel" it out with the "can" twice. Probably got 10 inches. Don't do this again.

El Skunko (Last one; three is enough)_____

Date:	October 28, 1999
Section:	Lower River; Peck to Lenore
Weather:	Rain
Air Temperature:	50 F°
Wind:	5-20 mph, gusty
Flow CFS:	3500
Rising, Falling, Steady:	Rising Fast
Clarity:	5 feet
Water Temp Start:	48 F°
Water Temp End:	48 F°
Colors:	
Fished With:	Pam Magers and James Gross

Comments: Don't fish rising river, low pressure and rain.

A Steelhead's Top 22 Favorite Tricks

1. Don't bite…anything.
2. Roll a few times—let 'em know you're there.
3. Attack when their reels are in free spool.
4. Wait until they give up and put their rods in rod holders.
5. Bite when they gaze up into the hills looking for deer.
6. Bite when they are using "the can".
7. Bite when they are anchored and have lunch spread out.
8. Slap the lure with your tail and get their hearts started.
9. Hit going upriver, they never notice slack line.
10. Just grab the shrimp. They'll think their lure quit working.
11. If hooked, charge the boat, they'll quit reeling and curse.
12. Jump a time or two, barbless hooks come out real easy.
13. If #11 & #12 don't work, run to a rock and rub on it.
14. In an emergency, run under the boat—"chines cut lines"
15. In a real emergency, run around the anchor rope…twice.
16. If all else fails, bite the line…then do #17.
17. Jump at least three times and show 'em the lure they lost.
18. If they get you close to the boat, spin like a top.
19. Stay outside the net and deposit the hook point in the net's webbing.
20. If they get you in the net, relax and slime up—they can't hold you.
21. When you are released, flip water in their faces as you leave.
22. Go back and warn the others.

"I only make movies to finance my fishing."

—Lee Marvin

Friends and Relatives I've Fished With

Rich Agueros
Dan Anderson
Steve Antel
Jack Babcock
Kurt Bilka
Don Bowman
Craig Brandt
Bob Capcovic
Diane Capcovic
Tim Coldsnow
Bill Cook
Milly Cross
Tyler Cross
Bruce Cushman
Blaine Davis
Randy Dawson
Cole Dawson
Chris Dunegan
Bill Eggleston
James Gross
Perry Gossett
Bill Guerhke

Judy Guerhke
Abby Hayes
Doug Hayes
Andy Hibbs
Chuck Higgenbotham
Marshall Jacobs
Steve Jordan
John Kelly
Larry Kerr
Stu Kestner
Gregg Larson
Mike Lemna
Tommy Linville
Rick Lubbers
Neil Lumper
Pamela Magers
Gary Mandick
Mike McDonald
Mike McKay
Jim Midgley
Tom Myers
Billy Myers

Bob Nuegebauer
Chris Oakes
Richard Powell
George Preszler
Bryan Preszler
Jeff Prior
Jim Rash
Cal Roy
Howie Shrupp
Tommy Shannon
Kevin Shellhammer
Mark Smiley
Jim Smith
Kevin Smith
Mike Smith
Nate Smith
Bob Turnbow
Mickey Turnbow
Rae Tway
George Whitaker

Acknowledgments

I sincerely thank the following people and organizations for their helpful and quick response in providing me data, answering my questions and granting me permission to use some of their copyrighted charts, photos, graphs and artwork for this book.

Eric Hulteen: Photo of "Dworshak Dam"
Mike McElhatton: Digital art "October Sunrise" and "Dreamtime"
Jim Wark: Air Photo "Canoe Camp"
Michele Dehart: Fish Passage Center "Steelhead Timing Graphs"
Alan Byrne and Russ Kiefer: Idaho Department of Fish & Game for the data they provided and for bringing me "back up to speed"-patiently.
United States Geological Service: "Water Flow & Temperature Graphs"
Bureau of Land Management: "Clearwater Sportsman's Guide"
U.S. Army Corps of Engineers: "Hatchery Photos"
Joe Tomelleri: "Spawning Steelhead" art on the spine of the book
Charlie Traut: For all his help on the logo and Nathan Billingsley
Kevin Colburn: American Whitewater for "The Selway" photo.
Pamela Magers: For proofing the first draft and telling me it needed more pictures because the book made her eyes cross.
Kathy Mullen: Final proof read; proving my grammatical inferiority.
Ginger Abbott: For taking a few months to put 18 years of my chicken scratch in a data base—then teaching me how to use it.
Kevin Becker: "South Fork Clearwater" photo
Nathan Billingsley: Cartoon & Diagram Artist. http://billingsleyconcepts.com

Dan's Fish Log© Comments

I have sorted this data every way I know that might provide information that is consistent and useful. The only pieces of information left are my comments at the bottom of each daily page. These comments are general in nature and not "sortable" except by date or fish hooked so I sorted by date for continuity.

I noticed anytime we were sitting around and somebody grabbed the four-inch-thick file that contained my fish log, they would just look at the number of fish hooked then skip over all the other numbers and start reading the "comments" at the bottom of each daily page. This usually produced some interesting and occasionally "colorful" conversation—particularly during cocktail hour(s). I sorted out three columns: the date, number of fish hooked and the comments I wrote in the log in that order.

I read it again and removed a few of the more colorful adjectives (nouns, pronouns, verbs and adverbs) and even a couple entire days (mostly Aluminum Hatch rants). I noticed the first four years I only counted fish landed so the "fish hooked" numbers in this entire book are slightly understated. These last 17 pages may mean little to you but there may be a few nuggets in here as well.

Date	#	Comments
12Oct89	9	Kelley is getting 10-15 a day from Peck - Lenore - Cherry Lane. Pam's said: "My arms are so sore I can't move them."
13Oct89	6	First 4 fish were caught prior to rain which started about 11:00. Pulled boat out at Gravel Pile, and put in Slaughterhouse about 4:00.
14Oct89	7	Very windy in Slaughterhouse. Wind coming up river. R.M. Turnbow got #1, Rick Lubbers got the next 5, Pam got #7.
15Oct89	2	Absolutely beautiful river like glass! One boat rowed thru Richardson's and on down prior to us fishing it.
22Oct89	4	Finally landed #4. First 3 charged the boat HARD and were lost. Nothing at Richardson's after leaving Slaughterhouse @ 2:30.
23Oct89	9	1st time fishing w/single hooks & shrimp on Hot-N-Tot--"THE Method" - "THE Method" catching about 2 fish to 1.
24Oct89	4	Fish still being caught everywhere.
26Oct89	6	John got 2 Zans-Airport, Mike - 4 Kamiah-61, Dan – 7 ,6 keepers, 1 wild. A couple of happy campers in my boat!
27Oct89	4	John got 1 - Richardson's to Slaughterhouse (when the rain stopped). Mike got 3 - Kamiah - 61.
01Nov89	1	John fished Pam & Rick Zans - Airport - no fish until 3:00 p.m. Banged one in upper Rich Rapid - 2 in Maniac at dark, which is now 4:30 p.m. (daylight savings time)
02Nov89	5	Started getting cloudy about 12:30 to 1:00. Fishing was steady on lower part after 2:30. Mike Smith had Jim & Gary. I had Rick, Pam, & Mickey. Followed Mike all day till 3:30.

03Nov89	3	Once it started raining everything stopped. Nothing in North Fork.
09Nov89	5	Had another hit @ tail out of Carbody. 5 to the boat, lost 3. In the boat 1 wild, 1 33" female. Caught 4 fish while ANCHORED.
10Nov89	4	River rising. Fished very low in holes.
11Nov89	1	16 checked in @ ISSU fish derby - 12 came from North Fork. Rick & Tim didn't get to Orofino till 1:30 p.m.
12Nov89	1	Moved to North Fork @ 2:30. Had 2 good smacks. Saw 2 caught on Blue plugs at Beaver Hole in N. Fork.
13Nov89	6	John got 2 in 1 1/2 hours at Black Rock on roe, saying Black Rock is a great hole in high water.
14Nov89	0	800 CFS not enough flow to even move plugs. Main river so high almost unfishable. Tim rowed the boat, Don't do this again.
28Nov89	0	Storm went through on weekend. Mon & tues both very cold & clear weather. Water temp dropped about 4 degrees in 2 days. No hits.
29Nov89	4	Main river 35 degrees. Watched 5 fish caught in top of Black Rock on bobbers & jigs. Landed NONE of 4 fish in North Fork. (2.5 hrs. N. Fork, 2.5 hrs. Black Rock Roe)
30Nov89	2	Saw 3 caught on bobbers and jigs in N. Fork. Both fish landed 14# female, 16# male, BOTH WHILE ANCHORED.
01Dec89	0	Most everyone we talked to had a fish on plugs, bobbers, sammies, etc. We didn't exactly bust our butts. Someone in every hole we fished before we got there. 3 hrs total fishing time. (Fish on: - NONE-El Skunko! All day, every hole, Hot-N-Tots

27Sep90	2	John's boat. 8 lb. Snivler, wild.
28Sep90	0	John & Mickey got 1 @ 4:30. 2 more at dark (7:30 p.m.) at Potlatch by signs, with Hot Shot-Pink then green, both 35's, No scent.
29Sep90	0	8:45 Upper Richardson's, Fly (Mickey)
03Oct90	2	Water level at Dworschak dropped on 10/1. John said weather was really crummy.
04Oct90	2	
10Oct90	2	Blew like hell all day - only fish caught
11Oct90	2	Beautiful day. Fish were in fast water off right point.
18Oct90	4	Rained all day - got very tired
19Oct90	4	Drift boat in front of us got 3 on.
20Oct90	0	Quit fishing @ 12:30 p.m.
21Oct90	2	Only fish Slaughterhouse. 20 minutes - Chris & Rich got wet and cold.

22Oct90	0	Pam caught one in the Wall Hole (hole below Peck) @ 11:45 with John.
02Nov90	2	
03Nov90	2	John, Neil, & George got 3...1-Zans, 1-Golf Course, 1-Richardson's
04Nov90	0	Rained all Sat. night. John, George P., & Neil had 3 smacks, landed 1 @ 5 Mile.
13Nov90	0	Jim was learning to row his boat, only made one good pass through Slaughterhouse.
14Nov90	2	Only fish of the day on ... weather cleared, spent way too much time in 3 holes, should have drifted larger stretch.
15Nov90	2	Fished the new Hot N Tot /Spin N Glo method. Must let fish take rod all the way down before hook set. Also had line broken in same hole had 6 other smacks. 2-Pink House 10:15-11:00-2 in "Mickey gets out" hole, 2 in Carbody.
04Dec90	5	Fish were HOT, all on the seam between the warm & cold water. All fish caught while anchored! Must have hooked 15.
05Dec90	2	Fish still on seam between cold 34 degrees, and warm 44 degree water. All fish caught while anchored. Hooked 12.
06Dec90	16	Ditto 12-5 except - I counted fish hooked today!
07Dec90	11	"

26Sep91	2	
10Oct91	6	At same time we hit fish, Kelley hit 3 fish in the hole below us. Bite is on 10:00 a.m. to 12:00 noon and then again late.
11Oct91	5	
17Oct91	2	1st day after storm.
18Oct91	3	Lost the end of my net! Make sure peg is in next time moron.
19Oct91	9	Did not fish 1 hole Peck - Lenore. Took out & went to Richardson's @ 3:30.
24Oct91	0	Had 3 smacks @ Lenore and the Barn Hole on Green & Red Hot-N-Tots w/shrimp. No fish hooked. Fish very timid. Just nibble, no "strikes". Fish were not aggressive.
25Oct91	1	So low above, plugs won't work. In 5 Mile, island showing. Fish #1 26" keeper. Mickey hooked 3 on the Power Drift. 1 above Saddlebags in tailout, 1 @ Black Rock on Steelie Spoon, 1 @ Brush Pile Hole.
03Nov91	2	Really cold - heater kept blowing out. Pam calling the Pink Hawg Boss the 'FLAMINGO HAWG'

04Nov91	2	The smallest fish we ever caught on Clearwater - 3 1/2 to 4 lbs. Wild male!
05Nov91	2	No hits in Black Rock or Pink House. Had both holes all to ourselves.
06Nov91	2	First day after upper river rose 12".
07Nov91	4	Best day in 5 days. Weather steady for a change. Mickey dubbed fish #2 the 'Fish from Heaven'.
14Nov91	2	Water was high & dirty. Visibility maybe 2'. River rose Wed., began to fall on Thurs.
15Nov91	5	Water clear, neat day.
05Dec91	2	
06Dec91	2	

03Sep92	3	Only spots on river where fish can be caught this early in the year.
02Oct92	1	
08Oct92	9	Fish everywhere - rolling, etc...
09Oct92	6	John Kelly & friends hooked 10 in same drift on Blue & Green 35 Hot Shots. 3 Very low in Barn Hole, 3 hole below barn on Lava Rock points, 3 in RUN below Shrimp Hole (low in run) - 1 right of 1st point in Cold Springs. Current too slow in Cold Springs to*
17Oct92	8	Fish everywhere
18Oct92	4	People & fish everywhere
22Oct92	1	Had 2 good hits in the Wall, missed both. Another guide caught 2 right on the end of our plugs drifting roe - just before we got our 2 hits. Lots of people on river. Fish "spooky".
23Oct92	1	Water is so low - slow & clear - fish are spooky
24Oct92	1	Went Clear Creek to Button Beach with Mickey - Mike had Pam & Ray
29Oc-92	2	Section: from bank @ Tunnel Hole (1 hr) & Trestle Hole (1 hr) then from Mickey's boat Black Rock (2 hrs) & Pink House. 12 & 16 lb keepers, released 16 pounder. Trestle Hole hard to fish from bank. Black Rock a (?) Pink House being fished HARD.
30Oct92	5	John - 4 - Kamiah - 61. Fish #1 smacked green Hot-N-Tot, went back through w/different color Hawg Bosses & got him. Fish turned on about 2:00. All fish in relatively fast water.
31Oct92	1	No fish in Stoddard, Bowling Alley or Mink. Slaughterhouse, fish very high. Boat anchored in middle by big rocks on right down from point.
04Nov92	5	
05Nov92	7	Roger 9 (5 Mile - Zans), John 4 in 2 hrs @ Zans.

06Nov92	7	Roger 8 @ 5 mile - Zans. Followed behind John all day (they got none @ Ford's Creek where we got 3)
07Nov92	4	Mike 10 @ Kamiah - 61. 4 other boats on drift - never fished Zans.
12Nov92	7	
13Nov92	3	below Corral Creek. First time ever on this drift. Holes in order below. Trestle, Nottingham's, "The Flats", Sure Fire (Rock), Corral Creek, rocks below Corral Creek, Last Chance real good, never got to fish it.
19Nov92	3	Quit raining about 1:15. Fish #2 hit Pam's plug, then took off downstream, came back up as Pam's line went slack and hit Rick's. Fish had both plugs in mouth when netted.
20Nov92	5	Really nice day - DID NOT GET TO FISH MANIAC OR SLAUGHTERHOUSE as boats were already there. Got off river @ 2:45.
25Nov92	0	
26Nov92	0	One hit around corner above ramp on right. (Thanksgiving Day)
27Nov92	0	Snowed all day. Had to "shovel" it out with the "can" twice. Probably got 10 inches. Don't do this again.

14Oct93	1	Had to go thru Bowling Alley Hole twice & change colors before fish hit.
15Oct93	5	Fish are in pods.
19Oct93	0	
20Oct93	3	
21Oct93	5	James had a fish when we returned from shuttle. Fish #3 jumped 7 X's. Fish #4 - James jumped up & cast from boat to rock on right - 30' ahead of where plugs were working-landed 15 pounder (became known as − "THE PREDATOR"...per R.M. Turnbow)
23Oct93	1	Fishing sucks.
24Oct93	4	Doug Hayes greatest net job of all time going down rapid in Mink Hole.
25Oct93	1	
28Oct93	5	Other good hits at "Hobo Hole" and Carcass. Ray's first Clearwater steelhead. Didn't even get to fish Richardson's.
29Oct93	2	(After Peck - Lenore, took out & fished Richardson's, Maniac, & Carcass.)
30Oct93	1	I didn't fish Maniac or Bill's.
02Nov93	0	Time changed, gets dark @ 4:30.

Date		Notes
03Nov93	3	Never seen wind on the river like that.
04Nov93	7	Still no rain - few fish. Fish thick at hatchery pipe. Could only hook 1 - had little time.
05Nov93	1	Turnbow got 1 @ Lower Peck, hooked another @ lower Tomahawk. Water 47 - 48 Black Rock down.
06Nov93	6	Half hour before dark 2 great hits in Carcass.

Date		Notes
08Oct94	2	Randy fly-fished.
09Oct94	1	Very (?)
13Oct94	1	Fly fished upper Richardson's & Carcass & Mink & Slaughterhouse
14Oct94	2	2nd fish "good hit".
15Oct94	2	(both fish were great hits). Only hits all day. Nobody catching fish.
16Oct94	0	
20Oct94	3	Bank fished Tunnel Hole, Zans, Upper Richardson's first. Broke line on all 3 "spiderwire"
21Oct94	3	Fish in fast water. Fished the Barn Hole late and got not a touch. Very windy. 25 mph.
22Oct94	3	Very frustrating. Only got a good hook in #2. Decided not to come back for a couple of weeks.
22Nov94	1	Worst season in years.
23Nov94	1	Worst season in years.
24Nov94	1	Worst season in years.

Date		Notes
14Oct95	3	CLEARWATER CLOSED FOR SEASON-CATCH & RELEASE ONLY-NO FISH LGD COUNT. Almost all "A's". Snake & Salmon rivers are EX. NOBODY FISHING
03Nov95	6	Turnbow & Ray hooked 5 on SAME drift. 4 in Carbody. Again, Clearwater has been closed all season due to no fish.
07-Nov-95	3	Fishing good everywhere.
21-Nov-95	5	Some w/o corkies on George's rig
22-Nov-95	5	Some w/o corkies on George's rig
23-Nov-95	3	Some w/o corkies on George's rig
01-Oct-96	0	
02-Oct-96	5	(2 other great hits)First 3 were wild fish. 3rd fish jumped 8 times!
03-Oct-96	5	White shrimp on green lure, pink shrimp on red lure. Fish were only in the SHADE.
04-Oct-96	5	Fish would hit NOTHING but red Rattle Tot w/pink shrimp.

		DID NOT GET TO FISH TOP OF COLD SPRINGS.
10-Oct-96	1	Did not get to fish but Cold Springs due to fly fishermen and bankies.
11-Oct-96	3	
17-Oct-96	12	Fished upper Richarson's until the air temp got to 43, then went down to Richardson's & hooked 5 on my fly rod (w/Hawg Boss). Had Stu Kestner (my shuttle) fight the last 2. My arms were tired.
18-Oct-96	2	Slaughterhouse had one good hit. Rained off & on all day. Weather change seemed to mess up the fish.
31-Oct-96	2	Mostly "A's"
01-Nov-96	3	Water 2 degrees warmer below hatchery.
02-Nov-96	4	Gradient is 4 - 5 degrees f. Fish stacked up until 2 OTTERS appeared after 3rd hookup. Otters rolled over lures, we never got another touch.
07-Nov-96	2	1 or 2 per day on both places fish hooked I have never fished before…
08-Nov-96	5	Absolutely beautiful weather. Pam's fish #3 was a 38" 18 1/2 - 19 lb keeper.
14-Nov-96	0	Only got to fish Pipe & Peck. Boats everywhere. Mostly "A's"
22-Nov-96	2	Saw 1 other caught at Black Rock on a sammie. Miserable weather.

30-Sep-97	1	(fish caught was a small 'A')
01-Oct-97	2	
08-Oct-97	0	Could not hold anywhere in above normal flow & high wind.
09-Oct-97	5	Pretty neat water 2 B's, 3 A's.
10-Oct-97	1	Fished behind Roger & Steve Hoskins half the day. Passed them at Bingo Hole & didn't get to fish anything but lower end & then just for 15 minutes. Had 2 other great hits, & did not hook.
11-Oct-97	2	
17-Oct-97	0	Mike hole hopped: 3 @ Pipe, 1 @ 5 Mile, 2 @ Barn, 1 @ Lava Rock, doing same things same way we all were.
06-Nov-97	3	River flooded out last week. Just went down, but still high (3500 upper river). Really only had 1 rod out all day.
07-Nov-97	1	Big wild fish - 3 jumps 100 yd. Run.
08-Nov-97	1	32 fisherman checked in @ GTE Tournament with a total of 3 fish. Mike & Chris got 1. Tyler Cross, 13, caught 1st steelhead.
13-Nov-97	5	River had been up since Sun.. Weather got clear & cold. River dropped & fish bit.
14-Nov-97	1	Biggest mess I ever saw. Boat insanity - almost run over twice. Only got to fish Peck & behind island @ McGill.

17-Oct-98	2	
21-Oct-98	2	Turnbow about drowned us at the Pipe as his motor broke had no reverse.
22-Oct-98	2	Nice day. 2 nice fish. ONLY SAW 2 OTHER BOATS
23-Oct-98	4	Great day on the river. Dan rowed except Rowaround & McGill when Mike rowed. Dan 15 lb. At rowaround. Eggleston 15 & 16 lb. Keepers. ONLY SAW 2 OTHER BOATS
27-Oct-98	6	(Note: 15 fish were hooked in two boats, my boat -2 rods, 6 fish. Mikes boat-3 rods, 9 fish. Very few boats on river.
28-Oct-98	5	5 fish were caught, but no further information provided than what is shown). Very few boats on river.
29-Oct-98	4	(Note: 4 fish were caught, but no further information provided than what is shown). Very few boats on river.
30-Oct-98	5	Lots of "take downs" - 12 maybe. Pam & Mike couldn't hook'em. Dan rowed. Pam's comment at end of day,"I've probably had 25 fish on the past 4 days. I'm tired of fishing."
31-Oct-98	6	No fish except McGill! All in McGill.
12-Nov-98	5	Chris Dunegan Limited by 11:00 Richardson's - Slaughterhouse, w/KC Construction crew.
13-Nov-98	2	Chris Dunegan skunked Rich - Slaughterhouse. Mike Smith 8 on Black Rock - Peck. Turnbow 0 - Peck - Lenore. Fish seem to be bunched up from Hatchery to Peck - so are boats! Still no significant storms UNTIL today.
14-Nov-98	2	River out of shape, went to North Fork
15-Nov-98	2	Flow so low had to work plugs by rowing side to side. Flow is OK up from ramp 200 yds. Main river out of shape.
12-Dec-98	10	River had just come down & fishing was great everywhere. DUE TO WATER TEMP fish were in VERY slow water. RIVER WAS FLOODED & OUT OF SHAPE FROM 11-15 TO 12-10 (WHEN I HAD SURGERY)
13-Dec-98	8	Same as day before. Fish in slow water due to temp. Would not hit red, green, black, etc... Out of 18 fish in 2 days, ALL on purple.
16-Dec-98	7	Fish in very slow water due to water temp. 5 Mile clearer than Rich. Fish hit black, Fish hard to hook.
17-Dec-98	5	Nothing @ Black Rock. Had 5 or 6 more pulldowns fish hitting lightly. Hard to KEEP hooked.
18-Dec-98	4	An absolutely amazing 5 days. 34 fish on in 27 hours of fishing. Big flood brought lots of big fish upriver. Great way to end the year!

24-Sep-99	5	Fished in tee-shirt and shorts! Fish 1 jumped out of water & landed on rock! Fish 5 hit plug on surface as I was letting it out. 3 of the 5 were 32-36" 'B's! Cool Snake aiding migration.
30-Sep-99	5	Fished spoons in fast water - no takers. Had shirt off by 1:00 p.m. Neat day.
01-Oct-99	2	Never fished that stretch before. GOOD water.
07-Oct-99	4	*2 other takedowns. Fish were deep in tailout right at where rapid started to roll. Had 5 great opportunities. Landed 2. All 'B's. (Had 3 others on.) Nothing in Black Rock or Pink House. (Bill Gurhke - 16 lb. On 7 wt. Fly rod)
08-Oct-99	2	Got truck stuck and had to be towed out.
13-Oct-99	0	Flow so low plugs only worked high in hole, Bill's Auto Body, and top of Carcass Hole.
18-Oct-99	3	Two big fish @ Shrimp, one on my "new" fly reel. 2 good hits in Barn Hole also.
19-Oct-99	2	Pretty slow. Both fish were small.... 6 - 9 lbs.
25-Oct-99	7	Fri, Sat, & Sun previous, Mike, Chris, & Steve hooked 0-2/day. Fish were NOT in fast water except #7. In slow "glassy" holes. Like somebody flipped a switch at 4 p.m. but we were way down river. I think there are a lot of fish downriver waiting for better conditions to move.
27-Oct-99	3	Need rain BAD. So windy (downriver), could not even stop until Casino Hole. Mike, James, Cindy in other boat, down some stretch
28-Oct-99	0	Don't fish rising river, low pressure & rain - unless you have to.
29-Oct-99	2	River kept getting TRASHIER as day went along - probably higher. Nothing at Pipe. River 48 degrees pipe discharge 48 degree no gradient.
04-Nov-99	2	Another bump at Stoddard and one bump at Slaughterhouse. Tough fishing - nice weather.
05-Nov-99	4	Never fished Riffle above bridge abutment above Peck. Great water, as is "Cedar Tree". Did NOT get to fish Pink House or McGill. Water rising, tough fishing.
11-Nov-99	1	
12-Nov-99	4	2 other great hits at Rich, no hookups. Probably nobody fished through here in a week. We launched in the fog. Kind of looks like Nov. 11. "B's" start showing up. Lots of 25" - 28" "Jack B's".
17-Nov-99	3	
18-Nov-99	3	SURROUNDED by boats after second fish.
22-Nov-99	1	Had 4 other GREAT hits on fly rod. Could not hook one at

		LOWEST point in Brush Pile Lava Slide
23-Nov-99	4	No bites rest of way down river

14-Sep-00	2	Spotty-previous Sat. flow was 3200. Mike & Chris got 6. Hottest day I've ever been on the Clearwater. Shorts & no shirt.
15-Sep-00	1	Fished only Black Rock & Pink House
21-Sep-00	11	3 & 4 and 10 & 11 were DOUBLES. Landed 3 & 4, lost both 10 & 11. A 'Top 5 day'. Fish were virtually everywhere and aggressive. Lost 2 plugs to broken lines! In 'slick' holes. No "chop" needed. About 50% "B's". Could hardly stay in Stink Hole for wind.
22-Sep-00	5	Didn't fish Casino for (2) boats. Started at Casino Creek-took out above old bridge. Fish coming good now Snake cooled. Weather "20 below normal".
28-Sep-00	13	Good drift in low 3000 CFS water. Shrimp Hole must be fished HIGH-too shallow low. Could have spent most of day in 1st 4 holes and taken out at Satellite Flats. Did not have time to fish marginal holes.
29-Sep-00	7	Peck could not be fished - anywhere - no current. Fish were anywhere there was current. DON'T FISH THIS DRIFT @ 3000 OR BELOW!!!
05-Oct-00	4	Water stained and cloudy. Been falling all week.
06-Oct-00	5	No fish at Pipe (no gradient). None @ Black Rock. Water still stained, but better than 10/5/00. Nothing at Peck...again...
07-Oct-00	8	Had 4 or 5 other take downs, broken lines on hook set (Dan).
12-Oct-00	7	Fish by myself until 3:00 and picked up Pam & James @ Bills. Fish 2 was a 20" Chinook. Rodeo @ Richardson's. Great hit @ Maniac.
13-Oct-00	6	River rising. Richardson's good again. Nothing @ Bills! Heather caught 1st steelhead - 14 lb.
14-Oct-00	0	River blown out - not fishing... OU beat K-state 41-31. 2 naps.
15-Oct-00	1	(*1 other hit) River virtually impossible to fish it's so high. Blew through Richardson's.
16-Oct-00	4	Great hit @ Cold Springs 100 yds below point. River almost impossible to row (Barn). Fish in Screamer on right & down low, same at Cold Springs.
19-Oct-00	12	Fish 4 & 5 amazing. Mike almost turned boat over under bridge as he stood up to use the can and fell over Mickey!
20-Oct-00	10	Another great hit at Golf Course Tailout LEFT. Abbey did great job on fish #2 and #10 after learning on fish #1. Nice day.

		Started raining at Bills-then not a touch.
26-Oct-00	14	First two fish were a double at the Golf Club tail out. Fish were everywhere. We almost had another double at the trap club. Fish bit all day.
27-Oct-00	11	No fish in Sure Fire Rock or Coral Creek. Fished Corral Creek, lower Corral Creek...WRONG!... Missed LAST CHANCE altogether. Once shade hit Bonsai all hell broke loose on 2nd row through!
02-Nov00	7	Shot to Golf Course...nothing...shot to Rich...nothing... 4 other boats in drift. Got past them @ Rich. Lots of pressure all week - prior to our arrival.
03-Nov00	5	Went past 4 boats to Rich - NOTHING AGAIN. Fish anchored high @ Bills. Fish 2-5 in virtually unfished water. Great hits at Golf Course and Lower Maniac. Nothing at Slaughterhouse. Again-fishing pressure killing us.
09-Nov00	5	Low clear cold water. NO FISH @ RICH. Great hits @ Golf Course, Bill's, Bowling Alley and Pipe. Could not hook up. Dinks (?) that would not come back as well.
10-Nov00	2	Fish #2 = boat at power lines, low and right. Plugs barely moving. Not many 'slow' spots to fish in this drift. Tough COLD WATER drift. (Kamiah-61)

25-Aug-01	11	*Deep 12' plus hole JUST below Rifle by "propane" tank - by first tree on right
26-Aug-01		Just fish 3 hrs and quit at 11:00 p.m. Too hot.
15-Sep-01	12	Fish were low in Screamer and at to 50 yards below Cold Springs. Hole between points at trestle. 6' deep. Broke rod over my side messing with Pam's fish. HARD hit on fly reel - bird nested it. Fish started hitting when sun got behind THEM.
20-Sep-01	2	Unbelievably slow. My how things change in a week - when nothing changes.
21-Sep-01	5	(*Note: Screamer was high above rock ripping across rapid by big pine tree.) Rowed fast ACROSS current good way to fish fast water you can't stay in (with plugs). Clouds really helped (the fishing). *See 'excess notes' for complete narrative.
27-Sep-01	6	Only drift fishable. Peck ramp closed. Water @ 2630 CFS @ Peck (900 @ Orofino). Couldn't fish Barn Hole.
28-Sep-01	3	(*Note: 9 other missed fish due to broken rod, broken lines, etc.) "Hooked" fish at Cold Springs & Cherry Lane & Blackberry Patch on Mag Wigglewort-red. Dan's rod, couldn't row and get to fish. *Same as 27th. 4 other boats in drift.

03-Oct-01	10	Used 8 wt. Fly rods & had 15 "pull downs". Fish nibbled before biting mostly, but a couple slams. Had trouble hooking & keeping on fish. Low water? Who knows, but fish are around - need rain badly.
04-Oct-01	9	Don't fish UPPER river at this flow. Fish were below cedar tree in last 3 runs. #2 where Pam caught 17 lb'r on right seam, #3 never fished before but left shore before point then across to right other point. Rapid below island at McGill a bit tricky
05-Oct-01	7	Would hit nothing but RED. Finally changed at Cold Springs. Got a smack on a Green Rattle.Tot but all fish hooked liked red.
11-Oct-01	2	Spent all day rowing to Lenore with John K. Wind blowing 25-30. 3' whitecaps blowing upriver. Didn't start till we were in Wall.
12-Oct-01	5	(NOTHING on red)...Cold day. Fishing not great, but OK, for rising river.
13-Oct-01	1	(3 other hits). First drift in upper river as we finally got some water - TWO DAYS PRIOR. Not many fish yet. Wait awhile before going to upper river. Takes awhile for fish to get up there.
14-Oct-01	2	(*1 other great hit at top of Carbody, 2 great hits at Lenore Points on left...none of 3 hooked). Rained all night-got a little murky toward end of day. River been rising for 2 days. Showed Randy this drift for first time.
15-Oct-01	0	(*2 other hits) "I I I I love a parade"...20 boats in drift. Couldn't fish but Barn & Lava Rock, and couldn't stay in there long. Flow good all the way through Cold Springs. Peck ramp still "closed". NEVER AGAIN will I do "Aluminum Hatch"
16-Oct-01	3	Everybody got 3 regardless of where downriver. Odd day. Got 35" Chinook low in trap club hole. 1st fish ever in HOBO. 2 good hits in Trap Club Rapid and Slaughterhouse.
17-Oct-01	2	Nice day except for wind. Water still stained. Fish sluggish.
18-Oct-01	5	Everybody hooked 4 or 5 everywhere. Clearing, falling, or steady river helps. Barn hole great in evening. Jet Boat in Bush Pile for 2 hours before us. Never got a touch.
19-Oct-01	10	Randy found 2 fish at Rip Rap on right going out of Carbody. Rained most of day. Barn Hole was awesome.
04-Nov-01	5	Water a bit high for this drift.
05-Nov-01	11	All females, 32 - 34" long….
06-Nov-01	14	(Note: fish were caught all day long. All males, 34 - 36" long…???? Amazing fishing - fish everywhere. - (14th fish caught at Bills...Hawgs & MagWart, Purple,Black, or Red/Black,

		shrimp and pops)
07-Nov-01	9	Fish a bit more timid but still everywhere. Little fish, big fish, males and females. Pam upon hooking fish #8 and yelled "Today I'm a fishing machine!" GREAT DAY.

10-Sep-02	3	Couldn't find out from Dworshak or Corps what they were going to do with flows
11-Sep-02	1	Spent lots of time getting Honda motor off bottom of the river
21-Sep-02	9	Great fishing - Silver Red bars the best
22-Sep-02	9	Fishing great - windy, kept us from fishing some places
24-Sep-02	9	Couldn't fish Pink House or row around due to moss. Fish only wanted MagWart, PERIOD.
25-Sep-02	13	PM hard to fish, low flow, upriver wind, last 4 fish from lower Lenore point down 100 yds. Never fished there before.
27-Sep-02	3	Nothing at Pink House or RowAround Hole. Moss mostly gone. Couldn't fish McGill or Saddle Bags or Cedar Tree. Got 1 fish in Hole #4 and 2 at Leaning Tree at Peck, above tree-quit fishing at 2:30. went to 5 Mile- 950 flow-too low for upper river-temp 56.
28-Sep-02	12	No other boats around. Fish seemed to be in groups.
30-Sep-02	4	Really slow. Nothing in Wall, Brush Pile, etc...
01-Oct-02	6	Fishing seemed to turn on with 3 fish in last two holes in two hours. Lots of good water fished by 3 people for 6 hrs to hook only 3 in the a.m.
02-Oct-02	12	Really awesome day. Fish in every hole.
08-Oct-02	5	1st up-river float. Do not float below this level unless you want to walk. (800CFS)
09-Oct-02	10	Great day. Starting to be too many people. Couldn't fish Lenore. Boat in Carbody for 1/2 hour before we fished it.
10-Oct-02	2	Boats everywhere. Started fishing at top of Saddlebags. 2 boats in every hole. Upper River 1080 too low to fish (in a boat). Quit at 2:00. Took great nap.
21-Oct-02	5	Got late start (Greg lost keys). 2nd or 3rd in every hole. Banky's, jet boat, drift boat in Screamer. Not a touch Cold Springs Cherry Lane. Water low clear-slow-we need rain. Every fisherman crammed in to same 3 drifts.
22-Oct-02	4	Had shirt off suntanning from 11 on. Traffic jam @ Peck ramp in the dark.Shot all the way down to Mike's Hole & got 2. NOTHING @ Brush Pile, NOTHING @ Carbody, NOTHING @ Lenore Points. Powerboats all over the place. Lots of fishing pressure in this drift.

28-Oct-02	4	Storm moving in
29-Oct-02	8	Didn't start till 11:00 a.m. Snowed till noon. Breezy then stopped. *River rose till about noon, then leveled - look when fish bit (time).
30-Oct-02	4	No rain. Upper river unfishable and in fact iced up when I left to go home Fri. morning. Did not land any.
31-Oct-02	4	So cold didn't even start till 11:30. Only fished two holes. Slush ice in upper river. Still no rain.
14-Nov-02	8	**See attached graph (attached to paper copy). Fish bit when flow and temp peaked. Very important when water is below 40. Bob Nuegebauer hooked all but the first fish.
15-Nov-02	5	Finally got water (rain) the past 3 or 4 days which broke up the ice, but still upper river too cold. Fish were not real hot after hooked. Probably my last trip.

25-Sep-03	3	(*2 other hits) Good hit at bottom of Screamer. "Bar waitress told us there were no fish."
26-Sep-03	2	2 other hits at Lenore Points. Hot, clear, no wind. Take down at rapid above wall.
27-Sep-03	2	Big fish. Randy got 4 @ Barn Hole right below us, and 1 at Blackberry Bush.
28-Sep-03	1	Started at 7 a.m., quit at noon. Canyon Inn-nice cheeseburgers. Tried early a.m. till noon float. No better than mid-day but cooler. Not a touch Barn Hole, etc.
02-Oct-03	2	Same pattern as last week. A few fish around before noon.
03-Oct-03	7	Mickey broke off all 3 of his fish. So John and I had no choice but to toast all Mickey's breakoffs! Good fishing.
04-Oct-03	4	Wind blew so hard we couldn't fish right until about 12:30. Hot. Need rain. Fun fishing with Mike & John.
05-Oct-03	4	They quit hitting Brads lures. It's Hawgs or not at all. Fun to take turns rowing.
06-Oct-03	1	Only fish on all day. Powerboat guide fishing Lenore & Carbody all morning before we got there, said he got 4.
20-Oct-03	2	A lot of "A's" over after 8-25 made 'B' run look bigger than it is. Boats & Bankies everywhere. Looks like everybody decided the Mon. after keep opened they wanted to be on the river. Bankie tosses his Sammy IN our boat. (Note-off river at 3 p.m.)
21-Oct-03	1	Same as yesterday without all the people. No current to fish where fish are at this flow.
24-Oct-03	6	Started off breaking a big fish off at Hobo when I tried to move the boat with the fish on in the rod holder. Then lost both fish

		at Stoddard. Then broke off a monster at Bowling Alley when I wouldn't follow him down river. Then had a flyrod hook one*
24-Oct-03		*(continuation of comments for this day) over the bow of the boat and broke it. 6 fish on, one landed, 3 good lures lost, and two broken rods...Unbelievable day. Pink House & Black Rock too mossy to fish. (didn't have a rod anyway)
25-Oct-03	2	Rowed Chuck's boat 54" R&B. Nothing like yesterday but TBR got its name today when Chuck broke a rod there on a big fish. So one spot, 2 days, 2 fish, "2 Broken Rods". Tommy also got a great hit @ TBR and 2 @ Bowling Alley.
03-Nov-03	3	Couldn't fish Black Rock & Pink House for moss. Took out & went to Barn. Weather moved through, wind quit & fish bit. **Water too cold to have fished upriver at all - 34 degrees is BS**
04-Nov-03	4	Took Mike's boat. Not a touch after noon anywhere. Mickey did good at Barn at dark. Very cold. Snowed like hell until 10 a.m.
05-Nov-03	4	Started at Tomahawk. Mike started @ Peck & went to Lenore with Bill E. Not a touch. Campers (literally) @ Brushpile. Mike got two at Guardrail hole same time we hit fish at Barn.
06-Nov-03	1	Another boat pulls in right below me at Lava. Never seen anything like it. I've had enough cold, river, cold water and combat fishing at every turn. No common courtesy from anyone anymore. River totally iced across from Orofino up.

23-Sep-04	1	7500 way to high to backtroll with oars!. Pam caught a 30 pound Chinook. Biggest fish ever in my boat.
24-Sep-04	1	6500 a lot easier but still could not hold at Brush Pile and Carbody.
02-Oct-04	0	El skunko. Randy and cole hooked 6 Peck to Lenore day before on Oct. 1. Bad decision to fish up top but I thought fish would be up there at 3000CFS.
03-Oct-04	1	Water perfect. Should be fish above Orofino but not yet.
04-Oct-04	4	Obvious thermal block in upper river. On these bright warm days fish were in the chop only.
05-Oct-04	4	Very Windy hard to row. Fishing good till noon when sun hit water then not another touch. Fish hit Mikes plug at boat reeling in and broke him off in Rapid above BP.
06-Oct-04	3	Clouds kept water temp down but fish still quit at noon.
12-Oct-04	1	Bright, hot and lots of Jet Boat Traffic. I got real sick with food poisoning and quit early.
14-Oct-04	18	Only reason to leave anywhere was to get down the river

		before dark. We didn't even fish the last two holes due to dark. Most spots didn't even have to pull up anchor after getting set to hook-up.
25-Oct-04	2	Could not fish below Bills for all the flyfishermen - in everyhole including Slaughterhouse.
26-Oct-04	3	Been a long time since I fished this drift. Very deep. Did not get to fish best spot at 5 mile.
27-Oct-04	4	Once again, all fish in one hole. Bill had another take down at Trestle Hole.
28-Oct-04	3	Randy did about the same behind us but got 4 on the far left at Corral Creek. We hooked -0- there.
08-Nov-04	3	Upper river 36 degrees so we fished down river. Nobody in drift but us.
09-Nov-04	7	NF Holes: A. Below rapid at top rt.- B. By Rocks in water on left down from "A" -C. Point on rt. across river & 50 yds. down stream from "B"-D. Point on Rt. w/ rock in middle of river-E. left pt. down below ramp
10-Nov-04	8	Fish were Very aggressive hitters - no "dink dinks".
11-Nov-04	2	Could fish nowhere else but these two spots as there were people everywhere else. (Veterens Day)

10-Oct-05	2	Very Low,slow clear flow. Fishing sucked.
11-Oct-05	6	Cloudy and fish were much more aggressive than is sunshine.
12-Oct-05	3	
14-Oct-05	2	So windy I could barely row. At this flow downriver, fish are much aggressive if they have no light in their face. On clear days it is really slow. Worst Oct. 14th fishing I remember.
31-Oct-05	16	PAM"S 50th B'DAY. Mike gave her a May West Hawg marked "FAB 50".....she hooked 8 of her 13 on it. Too late to fish Bill's or Carcass holes. Fish everywhere. Banged lots of rocks at this flow.
01-Nov05	4	Only fish hooked - 4 at Richardsons - not a touch else where. River rising fast and coloring up from day before's rain. Flow almost doubled while we were on it.
02-Nov05	4	Upper River got up to 4000 and was murky so we did not fish. upriver
03-Nov05	3	"
04-Nov05	3	Should have been better but visibity and stained water I think messed us up.
05-Nov05	5	Better than day before but water still stained. Never would have thought at this flow the visibiltiy would be limited.

09-Nov05	2	It was cold in the shade. Followed another boat all day. When water hit 40, fish turned on.
10-Nov05	3	Windy day - hard to row. Could not fish Wall, Brush Pile or rocks and point below due to other boats. Upper river 36 degrees so we fished downriver.

DAN MAGERS

moved to Idaho in 1982 and helped start the non-profit Idaho Steelhead & Salmon Unlimited. As a founder, president and director of ISSU, Dan spent years discussing steelhead biology, politics and fishing with some of the most dedicated anadromous fishery people in the Northwest U.S. From 1998, Dan kept an extensive log of his days drift boat fishing Idaho's Clearwater River which is presented here.